BUY THIS BOOK! If you are a lawyer who is already as busy and successful as you want to be, congratulations and keep doing what you are doing. Everyone else, literally, needs to buy, read and follow the simple steps detailed in Steve's book, "The Ambitious Attorney." These are practical, easy, simple and valuable steps you can start on today to improve your bottom line, indeed your life. I respect Steve's experience and perspective and I know you will, too.

~ Scott C. Anderson, Founder/Publisher Leading Lawyers Magazine

We lawyers have a disease. Steve Fretzin's philosophy and techniques are a powerful antidote. I engaged Steve hoping that his intensive training and coaching would help me accelerate the growth of my book with less time and effort. My expectations were exceeded. Since my time with Steve, I've more than tripled my book of business and was elevated to become an equity shareholder in my firm.

~ Neil Dishman, Principal at Jackson Lewis P.C.

Steve's book offers guidance and advice in a manner that is easy to read and execute. He also offers specific examples and sample language to make your business development efforts more efficient. I can say from personal experience that the approaches set forth in this book work. Following it allowed me to dramatically increase my productivity.

~ Michael Melbinger, Partner at Winston & Strawn LLP

Before working with Steve, I lacked discipline in my networking and forming of strategic partnerships to get new business. I dreaded networking. I dreaded "sales." As a female solo at the start of my career, I faced some pretty steep challenges, but with Steve's help he guided me to a path of discipline, cogent strategy, and more enjoyment of everyday networking.

All of this resulted in more business and higher quality business. Before working with Steve, my numbers were all over the place -- some good months, some bad. Now, I have a thriving business with my husband as partner in his first position post-law school. Steve has helped my husband and I achieve our dream of being our own bosses and supporting our family, while being the best lawyers we can be. Always available to chat and strategize, working with Steve is the best investment we ever made.

~ Amy Cramer, Founder at Cramer Law Chicago, P.C.

Whenever I pick up a new book by Steve I ask the question, 'At what point will I get hooked and not be able to put it down?' It's always with chapter one, but in the case of "The Ambitious Attorney," it was chapter one, page one. For years now, I have counted on Steve to challenge our attorneys to think in new ways—and he never disappoints. As per usual, I'll keep a stash of "The Ambitious Attorney" in my office—and they'll disappear like all of Steve's other books do!

~ Sue Robinson, Director of Marketing & Business Development at Chuhak & Tecson, P.C.

Steve Fretzin is an incredibly guy. His class and overall training were instrumental to my success. He separates himself from the others by truly caring and investing in his clients. He is committed to the success of each and every person that he works with. Taking his class has given me a new perspective on marketing, sales and networking. It was a great investment for me.

~ James Wideikis, Partner at Much Law, P.C.

Steve helped me focus and better manage my business development efforts. He also helped me grow my professional network with new ways to increase quality introductions to people and better ways to prepare, conduct and follow up for networking meetings.

~ Jay Nuttall, Partner at Steptoe & Johnson LLP

Other books by Steve Fretzin:

➢ Sales-Free Selling: The Death of Sales and the Rise of a New Methodology

➢ The Attorney's Networking Handbook: 14 Principles to Growing Your Law Practice in Less Time and with Greater Results

Both books are available on Amazon.

The Ambitious Attorney

Your Guide to Doubling or Even Tripling Your Book of Business

A Collection of Essays as Published in
The Chicago Daily Law Bulletin

Steve Fretzin

ISBN 13: 978-1-79161-136-1

ISBN 10: 1-7916-1136-2

INTRODUCTION

If you are an attorney reading my introduction right now, you are in the top 10% of all attorneys nationally who understand the importance of growing one's law practice.

Never before in the history of the legal profession have there been more obstacles to success than today, and it's only getting harder. AI technology, increasing competition and a shrinking legal spend continue to affect lawyers and their ability to bill hours and make a sustainable living. If it isn't impacting you now, it certainly may in the near future.

This book was developed over years, working day in and day out in your beloved industry to help attorneys who are committed to growing and maintaining a successful law practice. My goal has always been to help attorneys drive dramatic growth for their law practices.

However, if I'm being completely honest with you, dear reader, it's very hard to read a book and follow its tips, tactics and methodologies to the letter. Imagine reading a book on golf and winning the PGA tour. My suggestion for you is to try and get 5-10 really good ideas from these pages and execute on them to the best of your ability. If success is all about effort done intelligently, then this is the book you've been waiting for!

On a personal note, if you have a question or want to take things further with me, please feel free to email me at steve@fretzin.com or simply call my cell directly at 847-602-6911. My goal is to help as many attorneys as possible live the life of their dreams and have true balance in their lives. I hope this book will give you a new beginning to accomplish your goals and provide security for your future.

~ Steve Fretzin

FORWARD

Dear fellow attorney and reader,

It's not every day that a father gets to write the forward for his son's book. As a retired attorney of forty years, I did not have the good fortune of improving my business development by reading about and executing on the strategies and ideas conveyed in this book.

Back in my day, marketing, advertising and selling legal services were simply not discussed or in some cases, even permitted. A lawyer without substantial connections had to establish a reputation for competency, honesty, scholarship, achievement and concern for his or her clients' interests.

Although those attributes remain vitally important to a successful career, it appears that times have changed. What proved effective yesterday is insufficient today. Most of the successful lawyers nowadays are also the best networkers, marketers and business developers. It's a reality today that lawyers must go out and get new clients in order to achieve real success in the legal space.

In reading my son's articles and books, I was amazed at what a time-saver they would have been for me as a sole practitioner years ago. The business development skills that are needed today seem menacing, but Steve always has the answers. This may be the importance of investing one's "marketing" time in a valuable way, making prospective client meetings more productive, or building a brand to reach a wider base of potential clients.

Steve has spent over 20 years in business development and has perfected legal marketing to an art form. His successes are verified daily by his attorney clients who read his content, listen to his lectures and graduate from his structured programs.

As you may have identified, this book consists of a compilation of articles from the last three years that Steve has been a regular contributor for the Chicago Daily Law Bulletin. I hope you enjoy this book as much as I do and get great value from his guidance.

Besides all that, he is a wonderful son, husband and father.

~ Lawrence G. Fretzin

ACKNOWLEDGMENTS

I have many people to thank for this book. Of course, my beautiful and supportive wife, Lisa. My son, Andrew, and my father, Larry. My talented editors Sue Robinson and Emma Zelewsky. My clients and advocates: Neil Dishman, Jim Wideikis, Gary Savine, Phil Barengolts. Scott Anderson, Jerry Maatman, Amy Cramer, Michael Melbinger, and Jay Nuttall.

TABLE OF CONTENTS

Part 1: Business Development

Part 2: Marketing

Part 3: Networking

Part 4: Practice Management

PART 1:
BUSINESS DEVELOPMENT

CHAPTER 1

GOING FOR NEW BUSINESS? DON'T LET THINGS HAPPEN, HAVE A PLAN

Imagine it's Thanksgiving dinner and the whole family is sitting around the table waiting for the feast to begin. Unfortunately, something is different this year.

The table isn't set. It's barren, just a big empty wooden table. Now, as if things weren't strange enough, mom comes out with the most beautiful bird you've ever seen — just dumps it in the middle of the table! Then, she rapidly empties out the dressing, cranberries and sweet potatoes all on top, in one heaping mess. Everyone is truly mortified. Has mom lost her mind?

Now, let's come back to reality and discuss what this scenario has to do with business development and having an agenda. Well, if you are walking into pitch meetings without setting an agenda with your prospective client, you should think again about my Thanksgiving dinner scenario. It's very possible that you might be sitting at that messy table and not even realizing it.

One of the most important elements to walking a buyer through a buying decision is maintaining control of the meeting. While it might feel natural to pitch, solve and provide your rate structures, most rainmakers know that free consulting isn't the best approach to business development anymore.

The mantra that I teach my clients is, "Prescription before diagnosis is malpractice." Therefore, it is mission critical to ask, listen and learn before providing your fancy pitch. This is why establishing a win-win agenda for you and your prospect is so important.

Below, I've highlighted the actual scripting for you to use. It's incredibly powerful, just ask any of my clients who now close deals with ease.

Step 1: Make it permission based.

After taking some time building rapport with a new prospective client, you could say, "Listen, Terry, I know how valuable your time is, and mine as well. I thought in order to make the best use of our time together today, it would be OK for me to establish an agenda. Is that good with you?"

The important element here is to get buy-in from your prospect. The language is very important because it establishes the key point of "making the best use of our time." This is something everyone is looking for.

Step 2: Establish the time and make it uninterrupted.

While it might be fine for a good meeting to go on far longer than anticipated, what about the meetings that are not going anywhere?

The last thing you can afford to do is invest two hours with someone who is totally unqualified to work with you or has no interest. Therefore, setting the stage for a 45- to 60-minute meeting might be the better play. You can always let it go longer if things are looking up.

Also, you may want to subtly ask for "uninterrupted time" to ensure that your meeting doesn't get hijacked by a lousy cellphone call. These disruptions can totally sideline a good meeting. In this situation, you might say, "I know we had discussed keeping the meeting to an hour, Terry, is that still OK for you? Great, and I'm going to shut my phone off so we won't be interrupted." This is an easy way to set the tone for your prospect to put her phone away.

Step 3: Define the purpose.

While there are hundreds of options for this step, I'm only going to suggest one. Make the purpose of the meeting intentionally vague.

You would say, "As I see it, the purpose of the meeting today is to learn more about one another and see if there's a fit to work together."

The goal of this point is to show the prospect that only a "fit for both parties" makes an engagement work. It also sets you up on the same level playing field with Mrs. Big Shot CEO or general counsel. From my experience, getting into the weeds with your prospect on the various elements of the case in the early stages of a meeting like this is a huge mistake.

Step 4: Defining expectations for both parties.
If you recall, I mentioned the importance of asking first and solving later. In this step, we establish the order of events about to unfold. You would say, "To see if there's a fit, I'd like to start out our meeting today by asking you more questions about your situation (or whatever the problem may be). I also tend to ask tough questions, is that OK with you?"

So, you might get the "asking questions" part of my script, but why did I mention "tough questions?" The goal of the meeting is not just to learn about someone's problems, but rather, how urgent they are to solve. This urgency can be developed not by convincing, but by asking those tougher questions and finding the prospect's pain.

By gaining permission to ask the tougher questions, it may force you to actually ask deeper questions than you usually do.

I also ask, "What are your expectations for today's meeting, Terry?" as a way to keep her engaged and to make this agenda more collaborative.

Step 5: Define a win-win outcome.
Before getting into this step, I'd like to do a little setup with you. What's the worst outcome from a new prospect meeting? Is it when they say no? In today's

politically correct world, buyers hate saying no. Mainly because they are afraid that you might not take no for an answer and keep selling.

They've been oversold before and detested the feeling, just like you do. So, what's the typical response when you want to tell someone no, but don't want to deal with them any further? Yes, it's the old "I want to think about it" routine. If you hear this from a prospect, know that you are most likely not getting this business.

Now, that being said, we need to get to the truth with every prospect we can. Therefore, the best outcome for the meeting is getting to a "Yes, let's move forward on this matter."

Or get them to say "no," so you can both move on. For the record, I relish every "no" that I hear from attorneys. If it's not a fit, why would we want to work together, anyway?

As far as the script for this agenda, you would say, "At the end of our meeting, I'd like to suggest one or two possible directions. If we agree there's a fit and we want to move forward together, that would be great. Also, if we find that there isn't a fit for whatever reason, I'd like us to agree up front to call it a no and walk away friends. Does that sound fair to you?"

Now, if you're like most attorneys, you're saying to yourself, "I can't see myself saying or asking that to a CEO or GC."

I would respond and say, "That's too bad." Because getting to the truth and having a prospect be honest with you is critical to saving you time and getting to a result quickly.

This outcome also releases any sales stress that might accompany the meeting. Giving permission for your prospect to say no will help her to relax and trust you in the process.

In the end, the ability to get buy-in and take control of the prospect meeting is critical to success.

Without process, you're winging it. I rarely hear success stories from someone winging it. I hope you can practice and try this agenda out for yourself. It is truly remarkable the difference it can make in your meetings.

CHAPTER 2

DEVELOPING BUSINESS TAKES THE SAME PREPARATION NEEDED TO GO TO COURT

One of the easiest ways to explain how to be a successful business developer is by using the analogy of a lawyer conducting a murder trial.

While this might be a strange way to illustrate my philosophy on business development, I ask you to bear with me as I promise to produce a solid "ah-ha" moment for you before the completion of my chapter.

Imagine you are engaged in the murder trial of the century. The suspect is being held without bail and you are diligently developing the best case. In reviewing all of the facts, evidence and proof, you disappointingly realize that all you have is one witness.

This individual claims to have witnessed the homicide from only a few hundred feet away. Unfortunately, the witness is severely nearsighted, has a criminal record and is a notorious snitch. As the prosecutor, how are you feeling about your case? How will this case hold up in court?

While this may seem like a ridiculous scenario,

when we relate it back to business development, it can take a more serious tone.

To grow one's law practice, attorneys today must successfully identify evidence that a prospective client has needs, issues and compelling reasons to proceed with any matter. As you know, CEOs and general counsels don't typically leave their existing counsel without significant cause.

Your ability to identify the key factors of pain, fear or gain may be the difference between new business and wasting your valuable time. Here are three key areas that will definitely make you a better business developer and maybe even a better friend, lawyer or spouse.

1. Build a rapport first.

It's important for the jury to like you when you're trying to win them over to your side. The same is true when meeting with a new prospective client. Be sure to invest some time at the beginning of your meeting to ask some well-prepared questions and get her talking about her favorite subject — herself.

For example, you might ask, "I noticed your business was rated by INC. magazine as a top place to work last year. How did you build such a strong work environment?" Or, "I saw on LinkedIn that you run marathons for the American Cancer Society charity. When did you begin running for charity?" Being prepared and getting your prospects talking about their favorite subjects is critical to developing rapport and trust.

2. Qualify all prospective clients on the phone before meeting them in person.

Try to be patient and not scramble to meet with anyone who's breathing. Take a few minutes on the phone to ask some qualifying questions. After developing some rapport on the phone just say, "To make the best use of our time when we do meet, may I ask you a few questions to better understand the situation?"

Then dive in with some solid qualifying questions to better understand if there really is a matter here or not. Asking a few good questions on the phone will save you time, money and the frustration of meeting with unqualified prospects. Be sure to ask the following questions on the phone before meeting:

• "Tell me what's been going on?"

• "What are your primary challenges, frustrations and concerns about (their needs)?"

Be sure to obtain one to three issues on the phone. This will give you enough "evidence" to commit your time to meet. Also, do not discuss legal solutions on the phone! Get the prospect talking and feeling good about you and your ability to listen. Then schedule the in-person meeting to discuss solutions after you've given it some thought (even when she meets with you, ask more questions before solving or offering advice).

A good way to deflect her advances on solutions is to say, "Prescription before diagnosis is malpractice." Giving away advice can eliminate the reason for meeting, which is where the magic happens.

3. Prepare your evidence in advance.

When a prospective client tells you her issues, you should think of this as "collecting evidence" or reasons to work together. The more in-depth questions you ask, the more evidence there is for you to engage in a new matter.

The best advice I can give to any attorney is to ask deeper questions to better understand the pain points of your prospective new client. Your ability to uncover these pain points will directly impact her decision to work with you. Here are some questions that will help you to draw out proof that this decision-maker needs to hire you:

- "With regards to your legal needs, what are your greatest challenges, frustrations and concerns?" (Ask if you haven't already.)
- "What have you done to address this issue prior to meeting with me today?"
- "How much is this problem costing you?"
- "How has this problem impacted the company and you on a personal level?"
- "What happens if nothing is done to solve these issues?"
- "On a scale of one to 10, how serious are these issues we're discussing today?"
- "Who have you used in the past and why are you thinking of changing counsel?"
- "Other than yourself, who else might be involved in making this decision?"

Think of the power you will hold when someone shares her deepest fears and pains with you. This approach will not only make you a trusted partner, but it eliminates the need to storm in and pitch right away.

Most lawyers find it's easiest to sell by talking about what they know best, the law. There is a term for this, and it's called "free consulting." The best rainmakers today are the ones who ask questions, listen and empathize.

The same skills you use in the courtroom need to be applied in the way you conduct your business development meetings with prospective new clients.

By building more rapport, qualifying on the phone and taking a deeper dive when meeting, you will find greater success when doing business development.

CHAPTER 3

BEING YOUR OWN RAINMAKER IS THE BEST WAY TO SUCCEED

It's happening every day. Change. Just read the Daily Law Bulletin or National Law Review. New law firm mergers and buyouts are becoming commonplace. Law firms are looking more like a business and less like the Wild West. It's a reality that the firm you work at today, may not be the same firm tomorrow.

While that could be a blessing or a curse, the common theme on the street for every attorney still remains, "What's your book of business?" Why is that so important today versus in the past? Let's take a closer look at the facts so that you can make an important life decision this year.

Fact No. 1: According to a Law.com article, law firm mergers are happening at a record pace. Currently, there are approximately six to eight mergers per month happening nationally.

Whether you are on the buy side or the sell side of a merger, it may not matter. Many of these mergers create an opportunity to trim the fat.

It should not be a surprise that attorneys with a

sustainable book of business are not considered "fat." Doing good work for your rainmaking partner just isn't enough anymore. Without having your own clients and driving business to the firm, you may be setting yourself up for disaster.

Fact No. 2: Being a business development coach for lawyers, I find myself interacting with legal recruiters from time to time. They regularly indicate that staff attorneys aren't as marketable and get paid significantly less as an inbound lateral.

In speaking with Chris White of The Gunther Group, he said, "In our recent experience, compensation for partners with a book of business valued between $500K and $1 million at midmarket firms can expect compensation ranging from $250K to $500K.

Without business, compensation could fall 20 percent to 30 percent, and would likely be significantly less (40 percent-plus) compared to partners nearing $1 million in originations. Importantly, midmarket firms rarely seek partners without a book of business except when they have a pressing need."

What does this mean for you? While some opportunities arise from time to time for an in-house role or at another firm, the only real job security needs to be created by you. If you read my monthly column, you know there are many skills that need to be learned (and they are learned, not innate) to make business development easier and even enjoyable.

It's critical that you find internal and external resources to gain these skills. We are only one recession away from another 2008 when lawyers were being released and displaced at record numbers.

Fact No. 3: The American Bar Association released its Legal Professional Statistics in November regarding the lawyer population and it's never been higher. There are currently 1,338,678 attorneys nationally and 63,422 in the state of Illinois alone.

With competition at a record high, it's never been more important to separate yourself from the crowd. Marketing yourself and your unique set of skills is the answer for many successful attorneys.

Ask yourself, "Who's the most successful attorney in my practice area?" Then work diligently to get there in the next two, five or 10 years. Working on your business development skills and personal branding today will be critical to your future. The good news is that most attorneys aren't doing this yet, so by starting now, you can work to get ahead of the curve.

Fact No. 4: The baby boomers are slowly retiring and it's not going the way we all thought. In the past, it was assumed that an elder's book of business would trickle down to the service partners' book in the form of originations. In today's business environment, it's not financially beneficial or even feasible for the firm to give full originations credit when the rainmaker steps down.

Hiding behind the older rainmakers and waiting for them to retire or die just isn't a foolproof plan anymore (and it's a little morbid, too).

While it's possible that you are due some reward for all of your hard-earned hours with his or her clients, counting on that may be the kiss of death for you. Balance your time on billing and originating to ensure you're setting yourself up for success in the future.

As I mentioned above, utilize all of the resources available to you. Work daily to learn, execute and grow your own practice. If you happen to get some credit on a matter you've worked on in the past, it's just icing on the cake.

At the end of the day, it's really "You Inc." and must be treated as such. Developing your book and having your own clients is not an option anymore if you're looking for independence, security and financial freedom. Creating new originations may seem like a second job, but with focused learning and execution you can still have the balance you need to be happy.

CHAPTER 4

BUSINESS DEVELOPMENT LESSONS FROM THE PUTTING GREEN TO THE LAW FIRM

Over the past 30 years, I have played hundreds of rounds of golf, never thinking much about how it related to business development. I was too busy swinging away, just trying to get to the next tee box without losing my ball.

A few years ago I met a golf instructor and decided to take a few lessons. It was a good thing I did because it not only improved my game, it provided a supplementary experience that really struck a chord with me as it related to business development.

As an attorney, you've probably been involved in a "pitch" meeting with a prospective client. You may recall the nervousness or anxiousness felt around the idea of signing up a piece of new business.

During your meeting, you probably believe that the end result or "close" is the single most important element of the meeting. While your origination numbers may depend on closing the deal, there is another important aspect to running a successful business development meeting that holds the key to your success.

Let me go back to my golf pro and explain. After meeting and chatting with my new golf pro for a few minutes, he invited me on to the green carpet to take a few swings. He watched me intently for a few minutes as I stepped up and smashed a few balls into the range.

Finally, he turned to me and said, "Steve, do you enjoy swinging the golf club?"

Being terribly confused by his question I said, "What?" I simply had no idea what he was talking about. Fortunately, he explained, "You seem to be approaching each swing with the intention of getting to the outcome as fast as possible. You don't seem to be enjoying the actual swing."

I paused and thought about that for a minute. Do I really enjoy swinging a golf club or am I just trying to get it over with, hoping to land the ball somewhere inbounds? I then realized there was very little enjoyment in swinging the golf club, and I was in fact rushing each shot to quickly get to an outcome.

For me, this conversation was a real epiphany. If the sport of golf is all about swinging a golf club repeatedly, and I'm not enjoying the swing, then am I really enjoying the game of golf? Pretty deep, right?

At the time, I didn't have the skill sets to truly enjoy the swing. Therefore, I was only focused on the end result of each shot. The true enjoyment of golf is in the beauty and enjoyment of each swing. It then became clear to me that a better, more fluid swing will produce a much better outcome.

This is where the missing piece of the puzzle was for me. It's also where I realized how perfectly this scenario relates to attorneys and the process of business development.

As I thought more about the swing in golf and what happens in a typical pitch meeting, there was something unnatural about both of these activities. Just like my wild and harried swing, rushing to pitch a prospective client can lead to an unpredictable outcome.

A better approach would be to slow things down and enjoy conducting a successful business meeting. Instead of rushing to pitch and talk about yourself, you would build rapport and focus on asking great questions. You would listen to your prospective client's legal problems and not feel obligated to solve them on the spot.

While this might go against one's natural instincts to problem solve, it will be a refreshing change to focus on not solving problems. By concentrating on asking tough questions and uncovering a prospective client's pain points, there will be more urgency for them to hire you.

The enjoyment of the swing in business development is to be found in the relationship building and questioning process that allows us to truly understand our prospective client's problems, needs and desires.

If you focus your time and attention there, they have to believe that you are indeed an expert and someone with whom they should be working. Having your focus on the prospective client and not on yourself can only help you in developing a new client opportunity. It might also separate you from the other attorneys who are still hacking away with their salesy pitches.

As you think about this new process of walking a buyer through a buying decision, you can truly enjoy your business development efforts and take away the pressure to simply close the sale. When the process is all about the buyer, good results will just happen.

CHAPTER 5

TAKING SELLING OUT OF CLIENT PROSPECTING

As a lawyer, you probably despise the word "sales." This word has justly taken its share of lumps over the past 100 years as soapbox salesmen and carpetbaggers made profits off of uneducated patsies.

I'm sure the thought of pushing legal services on the people you know isn't an appealing proposition to you. Sound about right?

When comparing the differences between sales and business development, you must first look at the definition of "sales." "Selling" is defined as the act of providing a product or service in exchange for money.

For some reason this implies that you are attempting to convince someone to buy what you are selling. The traditional "pitch meeting" model was created to convince and motivate a buyer into making a buying decision.

This happens soon after meeting a new prospective client as you attempt to demonstrate your verbal and legal prowess. The majority of sales professionals and yes, even attorneys follow a similar path with their buyers.

In teaching business development for more than 15 years, I have found that the model for "selling" must change to include little actual pitching or selling. The key difference in the traditional model of sales and what I call, "sales-free selling," is that we must not present solutions and rates until we clearly understand the prospective client's issues, needs and compelling reasons to act. This is not an easy thing to accomplish, which is why most attorneys fall back on simply making the pitch.

In today's competitive market, making pitches too early can lead to providing free advice without ever obtaining the new client. I use the medical analogy, "prescription before diagnosis is malpractice," to help emphasize the importance of holding back on your pitch until you better understand the prospect's needs and motivation for changing her existing situation.

The skills involved in questioning, listening and empathizing are incredibly difficult to master. Here are some tips that might help you get on the right track.

Tip No. 1: Build rapport.
It's very hard to get information from someone who doesn't like to trust you. In the first five or 10 minutes of a business meeting, focus on your prospective client. If you did your pre-meeting research, use that information to ask questions and get him or her talking. Try to find commonalities that will bond you before moving on to business.

Tip No. 2: The most important question in any business meeting is ...

An effective approach to a business meeting is to invest more time questioning the buyer. Be prepared to ask 15 to 40 minutes of questions to ensure that every issue, need or pain point is uncovered.

Start slow with some basic background questions to better understand their business dynamics. Then, lead into asking, "What are your challenges, frustrations or concerns related to the legal side of your business?"

This question can be altered as you see fit, but the point is to ask about their issues to better understand how you might be able to help solve them.

Tip No. 3: If you find a nugget of gold, keep digging.

Once you have a few issues on the table, keep digging to find what the prospect's frustrations, costs and impacts are as it relates to these issues. One trick is to ask your prospective client to provide specific examples of their issues.

When telling stories, people tend to provide more details and get more emotional. This will build a higher level of understanding to determine if the prospective client is even a "fit" to work with you.

Asking great questions proves that you are an expert without ever saying so. Your goal should be to expose the prospects compelling reasons to change that drives urgency. As you might already know, asking questions is the single best way to comprehend someone's needs.

When I think about salespeople's methods in a traditional sense, I can feel my skin crawl a little. My wife will tell you that I despise being sold to more than anyone. The beauty of learning business development is that you won't have to "sell" anyone anything.

My clients focus on building rapport, asking amazing questions and qualifying whom to invest more time with or whom to kick to the curb before too much time is wasted!

The reality is that knowing more about your prospects saves you time from selling and chasing the ones that were never going to hire you anyway.

The best part about a sales-free selling process is how you will make the buyer feel. Not only will he or she like and trust you, they will feel confident that you are the right person to help with his or her legal needs.

So, forget being "salesy" and focus on walking a buyer through a buying decision. There's no better or noble thing one can do than to solve problems for others.

CHAPTER 6

NO GENDER BARRIER FOR BUSINESS DEVELOPMENT

In knowing, working with and interviewing hundreds of women in law, I've observed a fair amount of angst regarding business development and growing a book of business.

I have heard comments ranging from, "It's still a man's world" or "As a woman, it's hard to be direct when asking for business." Whatever the case, the reality is that there's never been a better time in history to be a female attorney than right now.

The New York Times published a piece back in 2016 that showed women overtaking men in law school for the first time ever. Look around you, women are in lead general counsel roles, growing their own law firms and hustling internally to become the rainmakers of the future.

If you're looking for recognition, opportunity and freedom from the shackles of a 60-hour workweek, be sure to make learning business development a significant part of your lawyer lifestyle.

To make this transformation of worker bee to business development assassin, here are three easy to implement tips that work for women in growing a book and taking your career to the next level.

Tip 1: Become an expert at time management

With the billable hour, family emergencies and personal obligations all weighing you down, it is critical to get organized right now. The easiest way to do this is to buy the book titled "Getting Things Done" by David Allen. I am a huge fan.

In addition to turning my life around, I have pushed his concepts to my busiest lawyer clients who immediately see results from his concepts. Without getting extra organized with your time, you may be doomed to fail as a developer of new business.

Remember, if you won't take the time to read a book on time management, how are you ever going to truly manage your time?

Tip 2: Learn or do something with business development every day.

If you truly want to get ahead in growing your law practice, you need to become a student of business development. An easy way to do this is to commit to learning or doing one thing every day to advance your interests.

A few suggestions might include reading a chapter of a business development book, watching an online video or attending a business development or marketing focused on Continuing Legal Education. You may also want to e-mail one contact, client or friend for a coffee in order to open new doors that may seem shut.

One of the best tools for this is LinkedIn. There isn't a reason why you couldn't look through one of your connections on LinkedIn each day to see what GC, CEO or HR director he or she might be connected to. By making business development and learning a part of your daily routine, you create an "inner-culture" for yourself that will elevate your game.

Tip No. 3: It's not about being a man or a woman, it's about being the best!

One of the greatest tips I can share with you is that there are advantages to being a man and advantages in being a woman in law. What you need to do is rise above that and become excellent!

Now, there are two types of excellent. First, you must become an amazing and dynamic attorney that people are impressed with. This one point alone can make your career. Second, you must have an approach to business development that will separate you from the pack.

While everyone else is in fear to ask his or her contacts for quality introductions into the midmarket, for example, you could have an approach that is effective to get you in the door and closing that new corporate client.

When everyone else is busy pitching, convincing and flaunting his or her legal prowess to prospective buyers, you could be busy asking, listening and understanding their needs and pains. The skills to generate new business are learned, but you have to go outside of yourself to find the answers. Feel free to go to fretzin.com or theoriginationstation.com for more tactical information.

As a coach and trainer exclusively for attorneys, I am in the unique position to see and hear things that you may not. Many of the women that I work with start out with the same concerns you might have about balancing family, work and relationships. In the end, you have to decide what's most important to you and where you want to devote time. If you can slowly work business development into that mix, you may see advancement on the horizon.

CHAPTER 7

UNCERTAIN TIMES ARE ALWAYS A GOOD TIME TO CHECK FUTURE BUSINESS OPPORTUNITIES

Whether you are a big fan of Donald Trump or haven't slept since his inauguration, we all have to admit that these are shaky times. Changes are happening every day, and your clients may be in need of a sit-down with their counselor.

Every time you speak with a client, there are opportunities that can be uncovered to help her, while also identifying additional work.

Your ability to execute and run an effective meeting with your client can mean the difference between having yet another year — or realizing an incredible breakthrough year!

The best part, it doesn't take much time to accomplish. You only need to have the skills to set up the meeting, ask questions and follow up to gain the traction you're looking for.

When meeting with an existing or past client, it's mission-critical that you actively ask and listen to get more detailed information than you may have in the past. Here's what you probably accomplished in the

past when meeting a client for lunch:
- Socialized and built rapport.
- Discussed current and past matters.
- Enjoyed a delicious lunch.

While those are great starting points, what about...
- Asking questions to uncover new and interesting legal issues?
- Uncovering opportunities to cross-market?
- Identifying quality introductions that could be made for you?
- Creating opportunities to be a resource for your client?

As you can see, the difference in these two scenarios is quite different as it relates to building long-lasting relationships, obtaining more work and truly helping your client to solve problems. Here are three suggestions that I work on with my attorney clients to make their meetings more focused and beneficial.

Tip No. 1

Consider setting an agenda on the phone prior to meeting your client. The idea here is that you can set yourself up to have a more impactful meeting before it has even begun. The key is to set the table with a game plan to help your client better prepare for the meeting.

One way to lay the groundwork is to ask, "So Barbara, before we meet for lunch next week, I wanted to set some expectations and goals for our meeting, is that OK?" She will be very agreeable to this. Then say, "Terrific. In addition to reviewing our current IP work together, I'd like to discuss your business as a whole to better understand the big picture for your growth. I know these are crazy times and a number of my clients are concerned with the state of things. Would that be alright with you?"

The point here is that you are setting the table for a more detailed conversation about her business to see the big picture and identify "gaps" in their legal or business strategy. This may lead to additional work for you, your firm's partners or your referral sources that you need to keep fed.

Tip No. 2

The next step is to come to the meeting with some great questions that may lead to additional work or cross-marketing opportunities. Try to keep the questions open ended and work with her responses to take a deeper dive if possible.

Here are a few sample questions and the possible follow-up questions that will allow you to dig deeper. In this example, I'll continue to be an IP attorney at a full-service firm.

• With all of the craziness going on politically, what are some of your greatest concerns as it relates to your business?

• Tell me more about that?

• Tell me more about the other legal work that you deal with that isn't focused on IP?

• How are they taking care of you and your sensitivity to excessive billing?

• Where are the key growth areas for the company this year?

• How can I help you to achieve those goals?

• In doing IP work with many international companies, many of my clients ask me employment and immigration questions. Tell me about the recent and future issues you see occurring in these areas?

• I know you've mentioned to me on several occasions how pleased you've been with my work the past few years. Who else should I be speaking with that might be able to utilize my experience?

• Would you be open to talking with him about the successes we've had together and see if he'll be open to speaking with me?

• Other than legal specific work, how can I be of value to you or your company?

• What other business issues are you having?

As you can see from these examples, there are so many paths that you can go down to find new opportunities.

If your client is open to these questions, you may uncover that she is dissatisfied with her other lawyers or that there's a blind spot in their business that may put her at risk. Asking questions shows a level of caring on your part because you want to learn more about her business and assist wherever possible. It's a win-win if ever there was one.

Tip No. 3
Ok, you've set the table and asked the questions. Now you have to follow up and discuss next steps. If there's

a legal issue, set up a follow-up call to review. If there's an introduction that's been offered, agree on a next step to ensure that it's followed through on. When dealing with an extremely busy client who has offered up a quality introduction, you may want to ask, "I know how busy you get, Barbara. If I don't hear from you regarding your friend Bob, how would you like me to follow up with you?"

This question is terrific for moving the introduction forward and having a unobtrusive way of checking in without bothering your client too much.

When thinking about your clients, it's imperative that you put them first. I'm sure we can all agree on that. Focus on asking great questions, listening and following through to provide the best experience for the client, while also uncovering opportunities for additional work and introductions.

These are challenging and unsure times for all of us. Our clients need us more than ever, so make the most of each engagement and you'll see greater results for your client and in building your book of business.

CHAPTER 8

THREE TIPS FOR YOUNG LAWYERS ON HOW TO BRING IN THE BUSINESS

As a young lawyer, there are a number of confusing and conflicting theories about business development and what role it should play in your life.

You may hear things from your firm's leadership, marketing department or colleagues that sound like:

- "Business development is nothing to concern yourself with yet."

- "You're too new to worry about learning business development. Just focus on learning the law."

- "Just wait until you make income partner, then you'll make time for it."

- "If you're not making money from your business development efforts, why bother?"

While there may be smatterings of truth in each of these statements, it's important for you to do your own research and make up your own mind about business development.

Making good choices is all about looking at the benefits for the time invested and deciding if you're willing to commit to the effort. If your eyes are open, it will be easier to see the path clearly ahead of you. To assist with this, here are three thought-provoking tips to help you understand if business development is right for you and how to get started.

Young Lawyer Tip No. 1: Be a great lawyer first
Yes, it's true. To be a great business developer, you must first be a great lawyer. Learning your craft is the single most important factor to shaping your future as a successful attorney. No matter what area of the law you are practicing, it's important to think about your future now and what type of law you want to practice. Here are three key elements to consider as you sharpen your legal skills:

1. Try to focus on the area of law that is most interesting to you. If you enjoy real estate, invest your time in that area. If you like to debate, focus on litigation. If there's something that you are passionate about, don't wait to get involved. While this might seem obvious, there are thousands of attorneys practicing in areas that are not interesting to them. When work is interesting or even fun, it can take away a lot of the day-to-day pressures that many lawyers face.

2. Find a great mentor with whom you can learn. Even if your direct boss doesn't have time for you, make an effort to find a strong mentor elsewhere. This can mean the difference between success and failure as an attorney and as a business developer. Having someone to talk to who has "been there and done that" will help you keep your perspective.

Be sure to meet regularly and ask lots of questions.

Most successful attorneys use mentors and coaches to help them to make positive changes throughout a career. These internal or external relationships also play a role if you decide to change practice areas or firms in the future.

3. Be a sponge! I've heard the saying, "If I'm not learning, I'm dying." So, whether you read the American Bar Association newsletter regularly, attend regular Continuing Legal Education events or listen to podcasts of attorneys speaking about the law, it's important to keep learning.

Some of my clients have built their reputations and books on staying current with the ever-changing legal system and laws in their areas of practice. Look into the future if you can and try to see what's coming up the pike that you can learn about and speak on before anyone else.

Young Lawyer Tip No. 2: Don't Sell... Network!
For most young attorneys, your job shouldn't be trying to close million-dollar deals with 60-year-old CEOs. It's just not realistic to do so. Rather, start planning and executing on a networking strategy to develop contacts that will lead to long-term business opportunities. Here are three ideas to follow in order to accomplish this task:

1. Failure to plan is a plan to fail. While you might have the best intentions, it's hard to get out there and network with all of the hours you are putting in at the office. Create a simple plan that allows you to focus your time in the right places with the right people.

Think about your friends, family, past co-workers and business professionals that you already know. Take the time to make a list and rank them based on "relationship" and "potential to help you." You may realize that you've got some terrific people to meet with and keep close to.

It's also helpful to set activity goals for yourself. You might want to take two breakfast meetings a week with these friends or attend one networking event a month. Try to use this plan to keep your activity levels up, even when the work is pouring in. There's always time to eat an early meal, bring in lunch or have a drink after hours. Scheduling the time is always better than hoping it happens.

2. Learn how to be an effective networker. In my experience, networking can be a huge drain of time and resources if not done with "intent." This means that you should study the art of networking and understand the best ways to proceed, rather than going out there winging it.

By selecting groups and events that are synergistic with your goals, you will have a much better overall experience. Do your research online or talk to your mentors before heading out to attend various events.

For example, if you're an intellectual property attorney, try to find a networking group with attorneys in other practice areas. This way you can all refer one another without conflicts. Or if you are focused on helping small business, try to attend events where the business owners participate. Try to find out in advance how many other attorneys typically attend to ensure you're not one of 20 in the room.

3. To get ramped up more quickly, try to network with the people you know best. Call up your high school, undergrad and law school friends to meet for coffee or drinks. When you meet, use that time to ask about his or her personal life, job and overall business. Learn what his or her needs are and see if there's a way to help.

If she's looking for a new condominium, make an introduction to a successful real estate person you know. Or help her find a new job if she's unhappy at work. In addition to making you feel great, you are setting the foundation for a cooperative business relationship in the future. Be sure to stay in close contact with the friends who may be able to use you or refer you.

Young Lawyer Tip No. 3: You're a millennial, use social media to stay connected.

While Facebook and Twitter are great for staying in touch and conveying messages, try focusing on LinkedIn for growing your law practice. Most business professionals are on it, but not using it for specific purposes. There are three key elements to being successful in leveraging this technology to your advantage.

First, you must develop a solid profile. People are watching you and you may not even realize it. Having a profile that is incomplete or inaccurate can hurt your image. It's similar to a resume that is riddled with typos. Invest 20 minutes and look at some creative and more elaborate LinkedIn profiles of your peers. Mimic what they are doing and update your profile until you reach 100 percent complete.

Second, develop an appropriate strategy for what you are trying to accomplish. If you aren't looking to meet or talk with anyone, don't set up a profile and stay off the site. If you are looking to get out there and promote your expertise, connect with the people who can help you advance your interests.

If you're like me and want the world to see you, be more open to allowing a variety of new people to connect with you. That being said, I don't want to connect with total strangers. Unless they write and tell me why connecting would be of value, I will usually not accept their request to connect.

The third and most important element of using LinkedIn is to use it to leverage your best connections to get quality introductions. The greatest benefit of this platform is being able to actually see whom your connections know.

For example, let's say I have a client who became a friend. I can go into his profile and pull up all of his connections. If there is one that seems like the perfect introduction for me, I could simply ask him what he thinks. Based on his response, I would follow up and ask him to make a call on my behalf to his friend and introduce me.

It's just that simple. I have been teaching LinkedIn for years, and it's been a proven winner for new lead generation for attorneys.

There needs to be balance in developing a strong practice as a young professional. Your direct income, job security and freedom may all be at risk without it.

While the emphasis should be on learning the law, and gaining valuable experience, you need to think strategically about your future as well. Start planning for business development now and you may surpass many of your peers in the near future.

It's not a sprint to the finish line, but rather a marathon. As long as you stay the course and work intelligently over time, good things will happen for you and your practice.

CHAPTER 9

HOW TO BE A BETTER PUBLIC SPEAKER — AND GENERATE MORE BUSINESS

Over the past 15 years, I have spoken about business development to help professionals obtain more business from their efforts. These groups have ranged from five people to more than 1,000. At the end of the day, there are two purposes to speaking that are paramount.

First, it's about building your name and brand to be seen as an expert in your chosen field. Second, it's to get actual business from the time invested. The unfortunate truth for many attorneys is that they may not be accomplishing either one of these goals.

Here are three tips that I help my clients with on a regular basis. In some cases, these tips have been game changers in their careers.

Tip No. 1: Choose wisely when deciding where to speak

One of the biggest mistakes I'm witnessing is attorneys who will speak practically anywhere to try to get their names out there and attract new business.

While this might be OK to try out new material or build your speaking skills, finding the right place and audience is really where the value is.

When thinking about your target audience, I always recommend two categories: First, the people who actually buy legal services like CEOs, CFOs and general counsel; second, the people who can routinely refer you to the people who buy legal services like attorneys in other practice areas, accountants, bankers and so forth.

While it's not always easy to get audiences like these, it's what you need to shoot for to build your book as a speaker in your marketplace.

One example of a failure to identify the right audience occurred with one of my clients about a year ago. He is a well-regarded speaker in the mergers and acquisition field. He's always out there speaking and sharing his words of wisdom. The problem we found was in his audience — other M&A attorneys.

Essentially, he was sharing his work, ideas and research with his competition, with the hope that someone would refer him. When I asked how many referrals he had received over the past 10 years of speaking to his peers, the look in his face said it all. Zero point zero.

Now, I'm sure there are exceptions where magic happened and big deals were landed with the wrong audience, but we can also buy lottery tickets every day, too. The goal with any business development activity is to hedge your bets by being smart and focused in your approach. Here are a few ideas to help

you find the best audience and venue to speak:
• Research your competition to see where they are speaking.
• Speak to other lawyers who regularly speak to find the best venues.
• Define a niche that no one else is speaking in and leverage it to get better gigs.
• Make a list of associations, groups and settings that make sense for you and call the leader to discuss a speaking opportunity.
• Create your own venue at your firm and invite your own clients and strategic partners to hear you speak. Have them bring their friends.

Tip No. 2: Develop a plan to ensure steps aren't skipped

One of the worst feelings a lawyer can have is investing a ton of time and energy into a marketing effort and watching it fail. Sometimes you know it's a bomb right away, other times you don't know until months later.

The reason most goals aren't met is because there was never a goal to start with. Think about it.

When the Olympics begin, do you think these athletes don't have a plan? What they eat, how they sleep, where they practice and who their coach is are all elements of winning. Jumping into the speaking circuit or continuing without the results you desire is simply not acceptable.

Developing a plan can be easy if you follow a few simple steps:

• As mentioned before, you must find the right audience and setting. Make a list of targets and contact them.

• Think about what you need to get together before speaking. This might include a solid slide presentation that's interactive, collateral material that includes your contact info or a survey that will be completed at the end of the program. This should ask each participant if he or she would like to have a more in-depth business discussion with you.

• How are you interacting with the audience? Don't read your bullet points! Tell stories and share analogies that connect with the people attending. Try to make the presentation entertaining as well as educational.

• Have a follow-up plan. It's too easy to collect cards or surveys and stack them on your desk for a week or a month. This is the single greatest killer of opportunities. These prospective clients must be called within 48 hours of your presentation, while they're still remembering how impressed they were with you. Don't miss this step!

Tip No. 3: Practice doesn't make perfect. Perfect practice makes perfect.

Have you ever heard that before? It's true and I can prove it. I was on the driving range two weeks ago practicing my golf swing. I hit a bucket of balls and then I went out to play a round of golf. The next week I did the same thing again. Have I gotten better from this practice? Of course not! The reason my game doesn't improve is that I'm practicing the same bad habits and swing every week.

When trying to get higher level speaking gigs, it's important to be regarded as one of the best. Not only do people understand your level of expertise, you become more desirable as a speaker. This means bigger and better opportunities to speak to the audiences that you want.

The best way to accomplish this feat is to improve your speaking skills. Again, reading your PowerPoint slides or speaking monotone to a group just isn't going to cut it. You need to be prepared with your content, practice it and then make improvements before speaking again.

I once had a presentation in front of a law firm of about 50 attorneys. At the end of the program, one of the attorneys approached me to compliment me on the presentation. It seemed a bit unusual, but he mentioned that he was tracking how many times I said "um" during my 75-minute presentation. Weird, right?

To me, this was an amazing compliment because years ago my speeches were littered with "ums" and "uhs." This was one of those practice and improve moments that I had after watching video of myself speaking. Back then I counted more than 40 "ums" and "uhs."

Regardless of your area of practice or years as a lawyer, you can make it as a speaker if you find the right subject, the right audience and if you work to improve your performance as you go.

Many of my clients excel at speaking because they've fixed the recurring issues that held them back. While speaking is rarely a quick fix for developing a bigger book of business, it can be a long-term strategy that changes the game for you.

CHAPTER 10

EFFECTIVE TIME MANAGEMENT FOR LAWYERS: IS IT REALLY POSSIBLE?

As a coach working exclusively with attorneys, no one understands the stress and demands placed on a legal practitioner better than I do.

Sometimes it feels like my entire day revolves around the demands being placed on lawyer's time. Not to mention the additional stress that's created when we discuss investing time in business development. It makes perfect sense why most attorneys shy away from their marketing activities.

Time challenges aside, you must know by now that nothing will have a greater impact on your personal and financial freedom than having your own book of business.

Therefore, it's never been more important to effectively manage your time to ensure you can fit in the billable hours and do business development as well. By the way, it sure would be nice to see your family, too! Here are three tips to help you improve the balance in your practice to create the career you've been dreaming of.

Time Tip 1: Have a solid plan for business development.

Other than doing nothing, the worst thing you can do as a lawyer is to approach business development in a haphazard fashion. Attending events, writing articles or even speaking can be ineffective if your audience isn't aligned with your goals.

You need to have a plan in writing to ensure you are spending your time in the right places with the right people. Think about the types of legal buyers and strategic partners you need to meet. Ask yourself, where do they spend their time? How do I get in front of them? How many do I need to build relationships with to really grow my book?

A good plan should lay out your goals, strategies and tactics to accomplish your objectives in the fastest time possible. Think of the plan as a car GPS. Before we had this tool, we would drive miles out of our way before turning around or heaven forbid ask for directions. Now the GPS tells us when we made a bad turn and how to get back on track. This is what a good plan will do for you.

Time Tip 2: Use your calendar to schedule time for business development.

You schedule meetings for a closing, deposition or a trial, then why not schedule time for business development. They are all important and need to get done, so treat them with equal importance.

Based on where you are in your career, how much time you need to carve out and your goals to grow your book, there needs to be an emphasis on carving out time daily or weekly for business development.

Here are three thoughts and best practices to think about:

• Look at your calendar to find times when you are less likely to be distracted by e-mail, phone calls or other people in your office. Not to boast, but I get into my office three days a week at 6 a.m. This gives me a solid six hours a week when I can get e-mails out, leave voice mails or make contacts through LinkedIn. If you're a night owl, that might be better for you.

• Once you do get meetings on your calendar, be sure to use the meeting invite tool to ensure that these meeting stick. Changing schedules and cancellations are sometime inevitable, however, we can curtail them slightly by getting into someone's calendar at once. If you're not sure how to use this tool, ask the person in the office next to you. It's become as popular as e-mailing.

• Use your calendar to schedule everything! If you have to make a call, write an e-mail or follow up with someone, schedule it. As I mentioned earlier, you need to start treating your marketing activities the same way you treat the law.

Think of your schedule like an advanced to-do list. The more you use your calendar to schedule things, the more you will actually do. Just seeing a follow-up call pop up on your screen will prompt you to follow through.

Time Tip 3: Always pick the low-hanging fruit first.

With all of the networking groups, associations and coffee meetings to choose from, you may quickly find your time drained away from you. One of the first things I suggest to attorneys is to look closely at their network and find the easiest way to obtain new business.

This might include meeting with existing clients to cross-sell, up-sell or find quality introductions. There might also be some family or friends who are in power positions, but haven't been properly tapped into yet. Whatever the situation, it's critical to leverage these contacts first.

A few concerns that you might have with this approach is the possibility of "blowing" the opportunity or "disrupting" the relationship. While this is always a remote possibility, here are some soft and gentle approaches that might ease your mind when venturing into uncharted territory:
• Be curious. You're a lawyer right? Use that as your excuse to ask a thousand questions about this person's business. Everyone has goals and challenges that they're more than happy to share with you.

Just be a great listener and ask open-ended questions to uncover possible needs. Then it might be more natural to discuss your value or services. By the way, "value" might be discussing the law in your office over coffee or referring them to someone else who can help solve a problem. Either way, you will have a much better idea of the opportunity for you to do business now or in the future.

An example of this would be at a family function where you see Uncle Dan every year. He owns a $20 million website company. You can ask him, "What do you love about your business?" and "What types of challenges do you have running a company of that size?"

Once you start Uncle Dan talking about his favorite subject, himself and his business, you can keep asking deeper questions to identify a possible need or a question he might have for you on the legal side.

• Ask for advice. In this scenario, you are looking to better understand the mindset of a business owner or general counsel as you are working to grow your own practice. Ask some great questions to obtain their advice and help. It's then possible that they might try to help you with your goals, make an introduction to someone they know or allow you to share your knowledge to help with a problem within their own company.

• Look to obtain an introduction from an existing client. Look, you're good at what you do and your client is happy. In addition, you've invested time taking her to lunch, a game, golfing, etc. Maybe it's time to ask for a high-level introduction to someone in her network that might want to have a similar experience.

It might make sense to schedule a lunch with your client, and before getting off the call say, "I'm looking forward to our lunch on Friday. I do have a favor to ask that would be really meaningful to me. I know you are well-connected and have been happy with my work. Would you be open to introducing me around to one or two of your business associates?"

This type of question is permission-based and should be received positively. The worst that can happen is that she will say "no." The best thing can be an introduction to a new client that could make your year. Plus, if she does say "no," it might be a wake-up call that you might need to work on your relationship building skills.

One way or another, you have to get your time under control. Remember, no one ever said on their death bed, "If only I had billed a few more hours." You can create a more focused and balanced approach to your practice by creating a plan, better utilizing your calendar and focusing on the low-hanging fruit.

CHAPTER 11

HOW TO GET YOUR NEW YEAR OFF TO A SUCCESSFUL START WITH 10 TIPS TO FOLLOW

When a year is fading in your rearview mirror, you may be asking yourself what needs to change to improve your marketing efforts in the new year.

In my experience, the key to success in business development is evaluating what you did both well and not so well this past year, and make some substantive changes to the not so well.

To help you with this, here's my business development best practices top 10 list for a new year. If you can execute on even two of these, it might make the difference for the coming year. Good luck!

Tip 1: Write a BD plan!

It might not sound like a tough ask, but 95 percent of all attorneys don't have a solid plan for growing their book of business. Without a plan, you may be all over the place with your BD activities.

Try defining your growth as it relates to new originations or number of new clients you would like to add. Then create two to four strategies or activities that will be a good use of your time.

For example, contact existing clients or other lawyers for referrals versus attending random networking events. Try to invest time where the low hanging fruit is easy to reach. Lastly, develop some actionable tactics to accomplish each strategy. This type of plan will be your GPS for the year. Be sure to track your activity to see what's working and what is not.

Tip 2: Get your LinkedIn up to speed.
I know, I know, LinkedIn is social media and who wants to get involved in that for business? You need to! Like it or not, this is your online resume for business that may be coming your way. Having a solid profile will help solidify your skills and expertise in your area of practice as well as building your personal brand.

Take 30 minutes and clean it up. Having a professional photo, expanded summaries and adding your blog articles will help to get you found.

Tip 3: Develop a client retention plan.
How do you keep your clients happy, loyal and committed to your partnership in business? Is this something you're doing haphazardly? Most attorneys do not have anything in place to ensure that they keep their clients close and happy.

My suggestion is to break your clients into A, B and C groups. Make the A's really happy by scheduling time with them monthly or quarterly. Schedule time to send them articles and provide "counselor" type of advice beyond the matters you work on for them. Maybe even find new business or contacts for them. My point, go way beyond the call of duty. Then lower the bar for your B's and even lower for your C's. That's OK, because you only have so much time, right?

Tip 4: Get organized with your time.

I'll keep this short. Time is money! The idea that you haven't read or studied how to be efficient with your time is crazy. Go online right now and buy the book "Getting Things Done" by David Allen. Read this over the break and follow it to position yourself to succeed in the new year.

Tip 5: Find the hot topic in your space and work it!

Think about how a crazy year impacts your space and leverage it with speaking and writing.

Are you an employment attorney? How about an article on do's and don'ts in the workplace. If you're a tax attorney, how about a presentation on the political climate and what that means for midmarket businesses.

Try to get ahead of things to be the first one talking or writing on new subjects. While most attorneys know this, few actually execute on it. Hmm ...

Tip 6: Create originations through cross-marketing.

For those of you in small, midmarket or large law firms, this is the no-brainer of the century. Create new business for the firm, get origination credit, while not having to do any of the work. Nice!

Commit to building relationships with three different partners who you can trust to refer business to. Then, when you're meeting with your clients and strategic partners, ask questions that might open doors for your partners. For example, if you're a litigator working with a CEO in the midmarket, ask about the company and see if there are employee issues. This might be a setup for your labor and employment partner. If you don't ask questions, don't expect to be referred in.

Tip 7: Stop pitching, selling and solving.

In my first book, "Sales-Free Selling," I teach the art of selling, without selling. This means we need to improve our asking, listening and empathy skills. The key to successfully closing more business is by allowing the client to buy into you, versus you selling yourself to him.

The next time you hear a legal problem that you can solve through talking, stop yourself. Take a few more minutes to ask detailed questions and learn what the real pain points are for this prospective client. Here's a good mantra to follow: "prescription before diagnosis is malpractice."

Tip 8: Be "the curious attorney."

When meeting with friends and family for the holidays, do a better job of asking questions about their jobs and businesses. If you can stay curious, you may find opportunities to help solve a business or legal problem.

You might say, "How's business?" Or, "What's new in the widget business these days?" Now listen. Then, once he's shared something with you, ask, "Tell me more about that?" The point is to ask, listen and be curious by going deeper. If you can uncover a problem, there might be an opportunity to help solve it.

Tip 9: Develop two or three new referral sources.

Again, you may know this already, but have you taken stock recently of your existing strategic partners and how they did for you this year? Just because you like someone and they referred you business last year doesn't mean she is on board with you for next year. Take 30 minutes and review your referral sources to determine where your business came from this year. Who was hot? Who was not?

If a few of your best and brightest have let you down, there are two simple options. First, reconnect and work together to get things back on track. Or, drop her like a sack of potatoes and find someone new to refer and get referrals from. By adding or replacing two or three referrals partners in the new year, you will have better success in your BD efforts.

Tip 10: Sorry to tell you, you might be an entrepreneur.
As the legal landscape changes and the emphasis becomes more and more about originations, you may find yourself behind in these skills. Make it a point in the new year to think of yourself in a more entrepreneurial way.

Focus on creating or building your own client base. Relying on others for work is so 2008, and we know what happened back then.

Develop better habits around business development to engage in something positive every week. In addition to building your BD plan (Tip No. 1 in case you missed it) and scheduling time, be sure to read, watch or engage in BD learning regularly. All entrepreneurs do this and you need to as well.

CHAPTER 12

CROSS-MARKETING YOUR LEGAL PRACTICE: SOME POINTERS TO FOLLOW

One of the smartest moves you can make as an attorney is to cross-market. While the concept may seem easy to digest, many attorneys struggle with implementation when meeting with existing clients. The idea here is to deliver additional services to a client beyond the one service you are currently providing.

Here's a scenario for you:
• You have a banking client and have been working on a litigation matter with her for over the past two years.
• Your relationship is solid, and you've been doing great work.
• This client has legal work far beyond the matter you are working on, however, none of this work is being given to you.
Why is that? The reasons may include:
• The client doesn't know that your firm handles other types of legal work.

• The client wasn't asked questions about the bank's business as a whole.

• The client has never met any of your partners who are highly skilled in these other areas.

• You never felt comfortable asking the client for additional work.

Whatever the reason, it's important to understand the value of cross-marketing and how it benefits everyone involved. One of the single greatest opportunities you have is the ability to bring in work and not have to actually do the work. While there are some potential downsides to this, with the right partners in place it can be a home run for you in building your book.

The main benefit to your client would be twofold. First, you would be the quarterback for your client in handling their broader legal needs. It's always best to have one person leading the charge. Second, you client's external communication would improve. Dealing with one person and one firm leads to better coordination of legal services.

What I hear on a regular basis as a business development coach for attorneys is that there is a lack of process and effective language to execute on the cross-marketing opportunities that do exist. My goal for this chapter is to provide you a tactical approach to cross-marketing in a non-salesy way. There are three steps to accomplish this task.

Set yourself up for success
Prior to meeting with an existing client, call her to set

the stage for your meeting. Let her know that in addition to catching up on the matter at hand, you would like to discuss her business as a whole and make sure that she is limiting her legal risk.

You could say, "Lately, I've been speaking with a number of my clients who have businesses similar to yours. Like you, they are all happy with my litigation work, however, there were other areas within their businesses where they weren't being properly protected from a legal vantage point. If it's alright with you, I'd like to run through a proactive legal checklist with you when we get together."

The idea here is to set up the conversation ahead of time to ensure you are not springing this on your client in the meeting. You bring up the subject as "other client's issues" so you are not specifically saying that your client has these problems and therefore not insinuating directly that she has specific legal issues or needs.

This approach is also permission-based, so you are confirming buy-in from your client on this specific discussion prior to the meeting happening.

Develop your six pillars and survey questions for your client

While there are a variety of practice areas that your firm may represent, it's important to think about the top six legal pillars that are most likely to carry weight with your business clients. The six that we see on a regular basis include:

- Labor and employment
- Intellectual property

- Estate planning and succession planning
- Real estate and construction
- Litigation and dispute resolution
- Business and finance

It is important to think about each client's business and to develop your own list of six pillars as the foundation for questioning. Once you have six pillars selected, work to develop one to two primary questions around each pillar that would engage your client into dialogue around that particular area of his or her business.

Feel free to start with some general "softball" questions like, "How's your business coming along?" or "What are some of the business issues that you dealt with this past year?"

Once you have a better lay of the land, feel free to get more specific to the six pillars. If you know that your client has a number of real estate holdings, for example, you might say "I know you have real estate all over the Midwest, tell me how that's coming along?" or "I know you've been expanding your real estate holdings over the past three years. Tell me about your future plans over the next three years."

Once your client has given you more information about his or her real estate needs or issues, ask a deeper question to open up the subject further. You could say, "It sounds like your growth is exponential. Describe some of the issues that occur with this type of growth," or "Who is handling this for you, and how is that coming along?"

The key here is to get your client talking about other areas of his or her business. Based on your initial questions and the follow-up ones, you may be able to uncover a business or legal problem that you could help him or her with. Try to use open-ended questions to avoid a yes-or-no response.

If you are truly interested in obtaining more business from cross-marketing, take the time to write down your six main pillars and the questions that you would want to ask. This survey could be the best tool you've ever used to develop new business. Statistically, it's much easier to obtain additional work from an existing client rather than finding new business.

Follow up

Once you've reviewed your survey with your client, it's important to secure a next step. If you found out that she wasn't 100 percent happy with her existing real estate attorney, you would want to set up a meeting with the best real estate attorney in your office.

Be sure this is someone you like and trust. Having skillful and trustworthy partners to introduce to your client can make the world of difference in effectively cross-marketing your clients.

If you're going to share your coveted client with one of your peers, be sure he is not going to steal your client down the road. To assist with this, be sure to set yourself up as the quarterback for all your client's legal needs. This will help ensure her relationship will remain strongest with you.

One of most important tactics to remember when meeting a client for cross-marketing is to never leave a meeting without a specific next step. Discuss the details with your client and include a date and time to speak or meet again.

Try to avoid saying things like, "Let's touch base in a few weeks to discuss this further." This is bad form. She is busy, and you are certainly busy. Not setting up a specific next step is asking for trouble in driving this new business forward.

Almost everyone has a calendar directly on their phone, so ask your client to schedule a follow-up meeting right there on the spot. It's not unusual to do that anymore.

The impact that cross-marketing can have on your practice is incredible. The keys to success here are to set up the meeting with no surprises, be prepared to ask questions around a variety of practice areas and to follow up right away to ensure the opportunity doesn't disappear before your eyes.

A safe idea is to try an initial run with a client that you are very close with. Explain that you have their best interests at heart and want to make sure he or she is well-protected in his or her business. Once you see how easy it is to bring in new business through cross-marketing, you will make this a priority in your business development activities moving forward.

CHAPTER 13

HOW TO PRIME THE BUSINESS PUMP: TEAMING WITH PARTNERS GOOD FOR ALL

In the previous chapter I explain the importance of cross-marketing legal services as a value-add for your existing clients.

For this next chapter, I've identified a few additional pointers that I believe round out the conversation and help you get real traction in the very important area of business development.

There are three key components to success when trying to proactively cross-market your firm.

No. 1: Know what your firm does and who you feel comfortable referring.

Before running out to cross-sell your firm, stop and think for a minute. What practice areas do we do that are most closely related to my practice area?

If you are an estate planning attorney, for example, wouldn't the obvious cross-marketing opportunity be with your tax group, real estate group or family law group? While you should be open to all practice areas, there may be a few that are more on the nose. As an estate planner, you are just less likely to run into class action, IP or big PI cases than other attorneys.

Once you've determined what areas to focus on, search out and meet with the attorneys you may be sharing clients with.

Now, some of the grumbles I hear from attorneys about cross-marketing relates to a few potential pitfalls that may occur during the process.

For example, giving a matter to your partner who, unbeknownst to you, may do a lousy job or poorly communicate with clients. Another concern might be your partner potentially stealing your client away from you.

Now, while these things happen from time to time, your first job before focusing on the cross-sell is to really vet the lawyers with whom you will be bringing in on your client deals.

If you know your partner very well and have observed how professionally and skillfully she works with other clients, your comfort level will go way up.

If you are meeting with new partners, get to know them on a personal level as well as professional. I had a business associate years ago that would talk negatively about others while we were having lunch. Not very trustworthy, so that relationship ended quickly.

The key is to meet with and qualify the partners that you believe will make you look good to your clients, while also mitigating the risk of having issues down the road.

No. 2: Get prepared with the right questions before meeting with your clients.

Congratulations on selecting a few solid partners to bring in to meet with your clients. You're ready to move onto the next step, which involves getting a list of questions prepared for your next client lunch meeting.

These questions will be critical to identifying opportunities for more work, without having to ask for it. Yes, you heard me right. You don't have to ask for the work. By asking questions and identifying areas of issue, your client will ask you for help! Nice, right?

To help you along with that process, here are a number of questions that you could ask during a lunch meeting to uncover potential business.

General litigation

• In business cash is king. How are you doing with collections and receivables?

• How are relationships with your vendors? Are they living up to their commitments to help your business succeed?

• How do you use noncompete agreements?

• How does your business protect confidentiality and long-term customer relationships?

Estate planning

• When was the last time you had your estate plan reviewed?

• What do you think would happen to your assets,

including your business, if you were to die without having an estate plan in place?

• When was your estate plan drafted? Any recent changes in your family?

• How are you going to transition the business when you retire? Does your plan include an asset protection plan?

General corporate

• Is your corporate book up to date so that your business does not lose its limited liability?

• Are you expecting any transactions that will impact the business and you personally?

• Do you have issues regarding employees, vendors or customers?

• Do you have a succession plan for the business?

• Do you and your partners have a shareholder or buy-sell agreement in place?

Labor and employment

• When was the last time your company handbook was reviewed?

• Do you have restrictive covenant agreements, or do you have a need for such agreements?

• Do you have any plans to hire or fire any employees in the near future?

• Any big changes to grow or reduce your labor force this year or in the next few?

• Do you have an employee incentive plan?

Family law

• How's your family? Everyone getting along all right?

• Any changes to your family dynamics?

• Between the business and family, there are usually a number of pressure points. Where are you finding the most stress?

Real estate

• I know that you are working to grow every year. Any expansions to your space or location?

• Do you have real estate holdings and how are they doing for you?

• Are you in a lease and when is it coming up for renewal?

Intellectual property

• How do you protect your name and signature products from being copied?

• Have you estimated the value of your intellectual property in the last few years?

• I noticed that you don't have a trademark stamp on your logo. Do you own the federal trademark on your brand?

No. 3: Execute on the right approach to successfully help your clients.

As mentioned earlier, the key is to focus on the areas that are closely connected to the work you currently are doing for your client. The questions above can be started just by asking about your client's business. A normal question would be, how are things going? Or try, what's the game plan for the next year to grow the business? Or, what are some of the challenges you are having this year?

The key is to be super interested and curious. Come prepared with a number of questions that might lead to identifying the legal or business risks she might be having. Once you've got her talking, keep digging.

For instance, if she mentions that things are great, but these darn suppliers are giving her the runaround, there may be some potential contract work or collections. If she admits that there's no employee handbook in place, you may want to ask about their turnover or risk for lawsuits.

Once you've identified a new matter, try your best not to solve it yourself. The whole idea behind cross-marketing is to bring your client to the table with the expert, which isn't you.

Just get all the details together, recap the problem or need for your client and tell her, "As it turns out, Barbara, we have one of the best tax attorneys in Illinois who I know can help you with this issue. Let me set up a meeting for the three of us and we can work this out with him." That's it!

As her attorney, she trusts you to help avoid the risks and hazards associated with growing her business. This meeting does exactly that and also helps you generate more work for the firm. As the client's one-stop shop, you will be able to help ensure the service and work product is quality while also making it very hard for the client to leave. Edging out the competition has never been more important than today.

So, let's wrap this up and put a bow on it. You have to get to really know, like and trust the partners you will be referring your clients. Then, you must begin scheduling meetings with your clients to ask questions and identify new legal opportunities or ways to help.

Lastly, you should be following through to introduce your client to your partner to drive the new matter into the firm.

Follow these guidelines and you will drive more business. The best part? You generate more originations and not necessarily more work for yourself. Win-win!

CHAPTER 14

RETAINING CLIENTS DOESN'T JUST HAPPEN; COME UP WITH A PLAN AND FOLLOW IT

In the Declaration of Independence it states that "all men are created equal." While this may apply to how we treat others with respect and dignity, we can choose to be more selective with whom we invest our valuable time.

For the purpose of running a successful law practice, all clients are not created equal. As a lawyer, a critical element to running a fruitful practice is managing your time in an efficient manner. How and where you invest your time can make all the difference.

Imagine that you're standing in front of an apple tree, which is loaded with fresh apples. Some of these apples are literally right in front of your face, while others are way up high in the tree. For the sake of efficiency, which apples do you go after first? The lower apples may seem like an obvious choice, however, many attorneys are still working entirely too hard climbing ladders reaching for those apples in the tree's upper reaches.

When discussing low-hanging fruit with my attorney clients, I always start with a discussion of their existing clients. Our goal is to uncover opportunities, which will produce the highest possible value for the time invested.

As we all know, before you can begin selecting apples you must first plant the seeds and water the trees. As this relates to leveraging existing clients, there is a myth that must be eradicated first. The myth is simple: if you service your client properly, they will be loyal to you. If you believe this for even a moment, welcome back to the 1980s!

Times have changed and so must you in the way you manage your client relationships. Statistically, it's six times more work and energy to find a new client rather than to keep an existing one. That being said, we all have to step up our game to insure that client loyalty is developed with intent. One of the best ways to accomplish this is to develop a client retention and loyalty plan.

Before groaning at the idea of writing a plan, I assure you this shouldn't take more than an hour to accomplish and can make the difference between success and failure in maintaining and building your law practice.

Here are the three important elements of a client retention and loyalty plan:

Step 1: Develop a list of your key clients and rank them as an "A, B or C" client. As I stated earlier, all clients are not created equal, so be careful in how you rate these folks. I suggest three qualifiers for determining what makes up an A, B or C client.

Ask yourself questions about each client and be honest.

- How good is my relationship?
- Is this a relationship that I can develop and expand?
- Are we friends socially or is our relationship more transactional in nature?
- Does she call me for general business advice or just about the deals?
- Have I helped my client in ways beyond providing legal advice?

Next, try to determine how much opportunity the client has to grow or how connected this client may be.

- Does she have a solid network of decision-makers that she can introduce me to?
- Is her company growing and expanding?
- Are there opportunities to cross-market and share work with my partners?

The last factor in determining who to invest the most time with relates directly to the amount each client has invested with you and your like or dislike of this client.

- Does this client invest a significant amount of dollars with you or did they invest almost nothing a few years ago?
- Was this client a complete nightmare to deal with?
- Did the client cost my firm money due to poor follow-through?

• Did the client continually question and argue my rate?

Based on these three factors and any others that you believe to be important, invest 20 minutes to create a master list of your top A, B and C clients so that you can move on with Step 2 of this plan.

Step 2: What you are going to do here is to develop a list of contact and relationship building points to help ensure that we are investing the right amount of time with the right clients. Based on their ranking, you are going to do more for the high-ranked clients and less for the lower-ranked clients.

To be clear, if you have a B that you want to make an A then be sure to increase the amount of touch points with that specific client.

Here are a few examples of different touch points that you can use to develop stronger and stickier relationships:

• Schedule a lunch or coffee meeting with your client.

• Go out for drinks and get to know one another better.

• Send a card on her birthday and for the holidays.

• Take your client to a game or concert. (It's important to know what she's into.)

• Call your client to see how you can help her business.

• E-mail or call your client to congratulate her on something she's accomplished (business or personally).

• E-mail your client with an article that is relevant

to her business. (You can use RSS feeds for this. Look it up.)

• Invite your client to a firm event or another high-level networking event.

• Be a resource for your client. Find her a new vendor, strategic partner or an actual new client.

Use these ideas as a guideline to create your A column, where a number of these type activities would be used. The B's would receive less contact and the C's less again.

For example, you might want to have lunch with your A clients four times a year, call each one monthly, e-mail each one monthly and find a solid contact for her twice a year. Again, the B clients would get less of your attention and time, unless you want to make that client an A-lister.

These are just a few of the many things you can do to stay in constant contact and help ensure longevity with your clients. The side effect of this activity will be to open up more doors for additional business and much needed referrals.

The stronger the relationship becomes, the less likely it is that a client will leave over price and the more open to referrals she will become.

Step 3: Scheduling time to execute on your plan is paramount to your success. While it's great to set up a plan like this, it's not worth the paper it's written on if you don't implement it. My best suggestion here is to find 30 to 60 minutes a week and schedule time as "client loyalty and development time."

Without making the time and setting it aside it will

never happen for you. There will always be work and distractions keeping you from this important task. Look at your calendar and find a spot weekly where you are least likely to be distracted or busy. You can even do some of this work on the train, in the evenings or on the weekends.

If you had to choose between retaining and developing relationships that already exist and have potential for growth or attending a local networking event and maybe meeting someone of interest, which is a better use of your valuable time?

There may be value in both activities, however, the later will bear fruit much more quickly when you've followed your plan.

CHAPTER 15

LEARNING HOW TO BE A RAINMAKER: YOU, TOO, CAN BECOME A MARKETING PRO

One of the greatest challenges for any attorney in growing a book of business is the genuine discomfort of asking for business from friends, family and clients.

Reasons for this may include:

• Fear of rejection.

• The impression of being too "salesy."

• The mindset that you wouldn't want someone asking you for something.

Sound about right?

One of the best ways to get on track as it relates to growing your book of business is to leverage the low hanging fruit that is all around you.

The best way to do this is by focusing on your best contacts and using some specific language to help you overcome the "head-trash" that you may be experiencing.

Scripting out a few words before making a call like this may be the difference between obtaining five new clients this year or none at all.

By the way, waiting for the phone to ring is not an effective and proactive strategy to growing your book.

Here are a few scripts that have been very successful for my clients to assist in obtaining new business from a friend, family member, referral source and even a successful client. These scripts can be used to set up the meeting beforehand or during the meeting.

The key to success with these scripts is to:
• Make the script a part of the conversation.
• Make sure the script is used in a conversational manner.
• The script should be permission based.
• Be sure to adjust and adapt each script to your own personality and style.

Script No. 1. A friend with whom you've never discussed business before:

"I was thinking that we haven't really had the opportunity to discuss our businesses with one another and it might be valuable to learn more about what each other does as new issues come across our desks. Would you be open to a lunch where we learn more about one another and see if there are synergies?"

Script No. 2. A longtime family member with whom you've never discussed business before:

"I'd love the opportunity to grab a coffee or lunch with you in the next week or two. We see each other every year, however, I don't really know a great deal about what you do. I'd love to learn more about your business and see how I can be a resource for you moving forward. I'd also enjoy sharing a little about what I do, as I know you run into people regularly with legal concerns. Are you free on ... [provide specific dates]."

Script No. 3. A lawyer or past referral source who you believe may have business for you:

"In addition to catching up next week when we meet for lunch, I'd like to share some possible contacts with you that might be beneficial to your business. I've been really focused lately on helping people who have helped me in the past. I'd also like to pick your brain for ideas on contacts that might make sense for what I'm doing. Is that OK with you?"

Script No. 4. A "happy" past or existing client who is well connected, but not currently offering you referrals:

"Before we meet on [date], I thought it might be helpful to think of some business connections that might be good for one another. As you know, I'm looking to meet (name a specific type of prospective client). If you're open to it, let's come up with a few names prior to meeting, that way we can both get more value from our time together."

Or

"I know you've been very happy with the work I've done over the past few years and I was thinking that you may know other business owners who would appreciate the high-level work I perform. Would you be open to discussing a few contacts with me when we meet for lunch next week? It would be really meaningful to me."

Or

"There's something I'd like to ask of you and it goes outside of my comfort zone a little, but it's important to me. I know how well connected you are and I was hoping that you'd be open to discussing some possible connections with me during our lunch next week. Is that something we can chat about?"

While there are many ways to approach the people you know for introductions, my clients have found that success happens when you try the scripts and begin to see results from your efforts.

Lawyers are always searching for proof and validation. Once you've been successful doing this a few times, your confidence will skyrocket and you'll make this a part of your marketing efforts every year.

CHAPTER 16

HOW TO BRING IN MORE BUSINESS AND AVOID BEING THAT FLASHY SALESMAN

When it comes to selling legal services, attorneys have a unique set of problems. Unlike traditional salespeople, most attorneys never wanted anything to do with sales.

You probably can't imagine yourself in law school saying, "Gee, I can't wait to graduate so I can start selling legal services!" It's just not in the genetic makeup for most legal practitioners.

While there is an inherent struggle that I witness every day in working with attorneys, there are three core issues that attorneys have that make business building very challenging.

Problem No. 1

The first big problem that attorneys need to overcome is what I call, "head trash." These are the fears and uncertainties that clog an attorney's brain as it relates to business development.

Most of us don't like dealing with salespeople and certainly never want to be seen as one. So why would you put yourself into that position?

The key to success here is to think of yourself as the top expert in your field. If someone needed a legal problem to be solved, you would be the best choice to call. Now think about all of the prospective clients in the marketplace who aren't happy with their legal representation, are overpaying or may not even realize they have a legal problem.

If you're not in front of them, they may not be getting the best. The key to removing the trash between your ears is by focusing on the buyers needs and not focusing on the pitch or the close. Shift your focus to the buyer and let them talk — while you listen. Be a good interviewer and uncover compelling reasons for them to work with you.

While this might be easier said than done, it's a critical point to being chosen. Buyers want to feel listened to and understood, not pitched or sold. Think about the buyer from this point of view and I guarantee it will help you relax and enjoy the process of business development.

Problem No. 2

The second big sales issue that attorneys have is time management. While this is not unique only to lawyers, it is one of their greatest challenges. For most attorneys, the pressure to bill hours is overwhelming. In some cases, one attorney might bill 1,800 to 2,500 hours a year. If we do the math, where is the time for learning business development, let alone executing on it?

There are two possible solutions to this problem.

The first is to work harder. The second is to work smarter. You probably guessed that the second way is the right way. Fortunately, there are time management guidelines that have been developed to allow busy professionals to increase their efficiency.

David Allen, the writer of "Getting Things Done," has been preaching these strategies for years, but mainly on deaf ears.

One of his main talking points is the importance of having a process for managing your time. No one ever said that "winging it" was a good strategy to be efficient.

One of Allen's mantras is the concept of the four D's. By taking information and plugging it into one of these categories, you can make better decisions about investing your time. They go something like this:

Do it: If it takes less than two minutes to accomplish, do it and get it off your plate.

Defer it: If it's over two minutes, schedule time in your calendar to accomplish the task.

Drop it: Say no to things that aren't client or prospective client related, and stop messing around online during the workday.

Delegate it: Get rid of anything you are doing that can be done for $20 to $50 an hour by someone else. Your time is worth much more than that.

Following these guidelines isn't easy, but once you start asking which D something falls under, you'll see the difference. You will discover where your inefficiencies are, and hopefully make improvements immediately.

Problem No. 3

Attorneys aren't trained to sell legal services. There are no classes in law school about selling and even the local and state bar associations frown on openly "sales-focused" content. In some cases, the only way for young lawyers to learn sales is from a strong mentor within their firm.

However, while the mentor might have the gift of gab or be a natural-born rainmaker, you are unique and probably not built for sales. For many attorneys, observing a strong originator doesn't necessarily allow you to learn processes that will work for you.

Some people are built better for business development than others. That being said, business development is a learned skill and not something anyone is simply born with.

It's important to find a sales coaching and training program to help you develop a plan with processes to achieve your goals. The alterative would be to figure it out by yourself, which can take years and cost hundreds of thousands of dollars in lost billable time and missed opportunities.

My recommendation to most attorneys would be to treat business development the same way you would learn a new language or play a new sport.

You must immerse yourself into it by finding books, videos and, most importantly, an experienced teacher who has a strong reputation for getting results for his or her clients.

Statistically, it takes 10,000 hours to become an expert at something. While we all know you don't have 10,000 hours to invest in learning business development, you might want to consider 100 hours as a launching point.

As a starting point, check out my last book entitled, "The Attorney's Networking Handbook." For most attorneys, networking inefficiently will steal away vast amounts of time because there's no process around on how to do it. This book cuts to the chase and provides tactical and actionable solutions to get results when networking. (You can order a copy on Amazon.)

While there may be hundreds of reasons why you might find business development challenging, the key is to remove that pesky head trash, work to improve your time management skills and really immerse yourself into learning business development as a part of your career.

PART 2: MARKETING

CHAPTER 17

FIND OUT IF SOCIAL MEDIA IS FOR YOU

As a marketing and business development coach, one of the most common questions I hear from attorneys is regarding the value of posting on social media.

Opinions vary on this subject to such a great extent that I thought I would create a social media test for you to better understand if it's a worthwhile endeavor.

It's important to be honest with yourself to ensure you make the right decisions with your time moving forward.

Social media assessment

Rate yourself on a scale of 1 to 5 (1 = not at all and 5 = definitely yes).

1. Do you have something of value to offer a given audience?

2. Do you enjoy writing and speaking?

3. Are you looking to grow your brand in the marketplace?

4. Are referrals important to your practice?

5. Do you understand the value of using social media?

Great, now score yourself. Here's the key to see if social media is really for you:

5 to 10 — You may have better things to do with your time. Perhaps focus on leveraging existing relationships and standard networking.

11 to 17 — With a little help and education, social media may be a good investment of time and effort.

18 to 25 — You're already on your way. Let's take this to the next level!

OK, now that you have your score, it's important to share the reasons I asked you these questions and how this may help you move forward to set social media aside for the time being.

Let's start with the first question. Do you have something of value to offer a given audience?

This is critical because social media for lawyers is primarily about education and updating your audience on the law and how it may impact them.

If you are not sure who your audience is or what you would even share with them, what would you even say on Twitter? As an attorney, you have to be an expert on your subject matter and speak intelligently on the subject in order to get value from using social media. Start there and then let's come back to discuss.

The second question relates to your enjoyment of speaking and writing on your practice area or industry. If you are not passionate about what you do, there's little chance that you're going to invest time speaking and writing on the subject. Some of the best social marketers are reading, writing and speaking on their subject, weekly, and it's impacting how they are viewed as an expert in the marketplace.

I would love our third point to include everyone,

but let's be realistic with each other. Building your brand in the marketplace is hard work. What type of effort are you really making? Approximately 80 percent of attorneys are worker bees focusing only on the work. While doing great work helps to build your brand, it's not even close to where it could be.

Becoming recognized first as "the" person to call for a legal problem is the epitome of success as a practitioner. Social media may be the best way to accomplish this, outside of kicking butt in court or making your client happy.

The fourth question asked related to referrals and their importance to you and growing your practice.

This relates directly to the point made above, while also leveraging social media to get in front of new referral sources that don't know you but read your posts. Being regularly in front of your audience will lead to referrals from places and people you never expected to hear from.

The last point might be the most important of all. It's nearly impossible to get value from social media if you don't understand it's purpose and how to effectively use it.

There are so many moving parts, it can be confusing to anyone looking to leverage it effectively. LinkedIn, Facebook and Twitter are different platforms. To help with this, let's talk about the big three and the key focus points associated with each.

LinkedIn
The most used business-to-business social media

platform. Most business professionals are now on this site, so let's look at the key terminology as it related to posting and brand building.

The main way to get the word out on LinkedIn is through posting updates or an article. This is a great way to share wins, new laws and your business point of view on your subject-matter expertise. Since you can't say you're an expert, you might as well demonstrate it in your writing and posting of content.

Be sure to find and use a dynamic picture and headline with your posts. The best posts are the ones that get seen, read, liked and inspire comments. Become a stalker by following and reading the posts of other successful attorneys. This will provide ideas and proven methodologies that you can spin into your own unique posting style.

Facebook
While this social network might be better for consumer-focused attorneys, let's not abandon the value of using it. CEOs, GCs and various referral sources are all on Facebook daily.

Building followers and fans can lead to new business if you stay with it and post interesting and valuable content. Developing fan pages, for example, can allow you to communicate directly with your well-connected friends and clients alike. Like with LinkedIn, it's important to utilize images and video to engage your audience and get discussions going with your base.

Twitter

You're either a part of the conversation or you're not. Twitter allows you to have a voice in the marketplace that you can control. Are you going to share humorous observations or broadcast industry information that's educational or thoughtful?

While posting comments is helpful to get your brand out there, most experts agree that Twitter is best used to engage your clients and potential strategic partners in a dialogue. Again, you are controlling the conversation or, oblivious, that there's even one to be had?

As you can imagine, it's difficult to write on a subject and summarize it down to a Daily Law Bulletin article. My hope is that it helps you think more strategically about social media and whether you should be using it or not.

Don't get overwhelmed, as there are outlets to outsource social media if you want help or don't have time to get directly involved. Many lawyers and law firms outsource to companies like mine to help take the pressure off, but we still need direction and engagement from you to make it work.

Right now, content is king. This means that you're either visible and growing or hidden and shrinking. Think of the world and how it's changed in the past two years.

As an attorney, growing your brand and driving originations has never been more important. Based on your score, it might be time to get educated on social media to take it to the next level.

CHAPTER 18

E-MAIL MARKETING: CONSTANT AND STEADY

I am asked almost daily about the benefits of e-mail marketing and newsletters. While I'm a huge advocate of this type of marketing, it's not always a fit for every lawyer or law firm.

Typically, I ask a few questions that help identify if there's value in expending limited resources on this marketing endeavor.

• Do you have 100 or more people to keep in touch with?

• Do you have something new or important to communicate?

• Are you looking to keep your clients and develop new ones?

If the answer is yes to any one of these questions, then please keep reading. If the answer is no, it may be because you are just starting out, you're in a "worker bee" role at your firm or you are close to retirement and looking to slow things down.

For all those who answered affirmatively, here are the top five reasons an e-mail newsletter would be of great value to you in sustaining and growing your practice. Also, be sure to read the last paragraph if you're serious about executing on an effective e-mail campaign.

Stay top of mind

Having something to e-mail your clients, colleagues and friends each month to keep in touch is rarely a losing proposition. Think about it, how long does it take to e-mail 100 to 1,000 people each month? You and I both know you don't have time not to do that. An e-mail newsletter allows you to get your name and important content in front of your people, your clients, on a regular basis, where you alone cannot.

One of the main reasons attorneys lose clients today is lack of regular communication and face time. Statistically, it takes six times more energy, money and time to find a new client, than it does to keep the one you have.

Building brand equity

I wrote earlier about the importance of being a leader in your field and growing your brand equity. There's no reason why that can't be done through your monthly newsletter.

Here's an opportunity to take your finest ideas, strongest wins, insightful articles and best resources and share them with your clients, strategic partners and colleagues.

In addition to adding value to these existing relationships, you're demonstrating why they need you in their life. This is also where word of mouth is key. Your audience members forward your material to their audiences, who then do the same. It's amazing how people love to share great content that benefits others.

Promote what's new

Do you have a new logo? New area of focus? New white paper? New win in appellate court? People love new! It's exciting to read about positive changes that people are making in their business and personal lives. For example, let's say that you share a favorable decision in court. One of your past clients sees this and decides to call you for a similar matter she is dealing with. Now you may get a client back that's been dormant for years. Nice, right?

Better quality leads

What's the easiest way to find new business? Networking? Cold calling? Attending conferences? The answer is "no, no and no." As I mentioned, the best way to get new business is from your existing clients and strategic partnerships.

What e-mail marketing can offer you is prequalified business leads. Again, the people who already know you and know your work are the most likely to use you again and refer you to others. While I'm not suggesting that these other marketing efforts aren't worthwhile, statistically they are less likely to convert and take much longer to vet.

Generate more website traffic

The final point I'll make on e-mail marketing is the importance of driving traffic to your website. That being said, if your website is terrible and outdated, you can skip to the end of my article.

A bad or outdated website will typically turn away business, rather than generate it. For those who have successful and well thought out websites, it's of critical importance to get people there. This is where you house your blog, bio, testimonials and other relevant information that can convert your network into new or repeat business. Your e-mail newsletter can do just that, leading people down a path and getting that phone call you are looking for.

Now, you might be thinking, "What the #$@! do I know about setting up a newsletter, let alone how it works to drive business?" Well, there are two options you have for this. First, go online and research options for automation tools like Mail Chimp or Constant Contact.

They will provide many videos and articles on how to do this. But, if you are strapped for time and do not want to learn this, let alone execute on this, there are many companies that actively take this over for you.

Like your website, your newsletter is an extension of you and your brand. If you decide to outsource this service, be sure you meet with an expert who understands your business and practice and that you can trust to get this marketing piece done properly.

CHAPTER 19

LAW FIRM WEBSITES: BASIC BROCHURE OR BRANDING TOOL FOR SUCCESS?

Recently, I was reviewing a law firm's website with the managing partner to discuss his thoughts on the existing platform. He looked at his site and without hesitation said, "I think it's fine." This answer is not uncommon as websites from the 1990s and 2000s are used every day in the legal profession to share the most basic of information with whomever may stumble across it.

Unfortunately, this managing partner, like most, is totally lost on the value of a good website and how it acts as a culture shifter, business generator and brand builder for a law firm.

A simple way to understand whether it's time to update your website is to ask yourself the following questions. Just check answer "yes" or "no." Once completed, we can move on to discuss the real benefits of this seemingly scary and possibly daunting investment.

1. Does my website separate my firm from other law firms who sell similar services?
2. When my clients go to my website, is there

relevant legal and business content to share with them?

3. Would my website attract a new (and younger) attorney to come work here?

4. Am I happy with the current culture of our firm? For instance, are we working in silos, afraid to share clients? Are we actively promoting our diversity? Are we actively promoting our goodwill and public interest?

5. Does our website deliver high-level prospective clients with more work (not to mention more from your existing clients)?

If you answered "no" to most of these questions, this should be a wake-up call for you to consider investing in fixing these troubled areas. To help educate you on this complicated subject and to ensure you don't overspend, I'm going to answer these questions for you now.

1. Does my website separate my firm from other law firms who sell similar services?

The book "Blue Ocean Strategy" by W. Chan Kim and Renee Mauborgne states that the sea is bloody red with competition and that the key to sustainable success to find the open blue waters.

A unique and well-designed website can do that for you. Let's say you are competing for a new litigation matter and the prospective client views your old worn-out website versus a creative content-rich site. All other things being even, which would they choose to handle their complicated matter?

While this might not have been important 10 years ago, today it's of critical importance. It's how people make informed decisions. Would you go to a restaurant that had images online that were severely outdated and appeared dirty?

2. When my clients go to my website, is there relevant content to share with them?

In business, cash is king. In marketing, content is king! This is the new reality that we all live in. Having up-to-date, expertly written content is more critical than ever to growing your brand and driving traffic to your business.

Having your own blog on your site, for example, can be a game-changer in your space. Not only will you be better known as a serious player, it will help drive clients and new prospective clients to your website — and to you!

Think about it this way — your website is face-to-face with your audience at moments when you are not. A well-designed website allows you to have 24/7 control of both your messages and your audience's perception of you. In sum, the website is working even when you're not.

3. What does my website say about the firm that would attract a new attorney to come work here?

Picture this. You are paying a recruiter 20 percent to find you a qualified attorney with $500,000 in portable business. This attorney would be an incredible catch for your firm. She interviews and is considering two other firms in addition to yours. Is it possible that when she researches your firm and sees an old-fashioned website that lacks diversity, she may go a different direction? Of course! You may not even realize that this is happening.

The 30- and 40-year-olds are the future of your business, and they are hyper-focused and critical on websites that are old and outdated. Your website can be the best recruiting tool for your firm when done properly. One good and profitable hire could literally pay for your site for years to come.

4. Am I happy with the current culture of our firm? Are we working in silos, afraid to share clients? Are we actively promoting our diversity? Are we actively promoting our goodwill and public interest?

Just like your clothes reflect your style, websites reflect the expertise and culture of your firm. Sometimes we need to reinvest in how we look to stay relevant with the times. Improving your website won't necessarily fix a bad culture, but it could.

The key here is that the fish may stink from the head down. This means that your top players need to be the drivers behind a fresh and new marketing initiative.

Without this support, the investment may not be fully utilized to grow business moving forward. If you can get the team behind a new look and approach to marketing and business development, it will help to improve productivity and positivity in the office.

5. Does our website deliver high-level prospective clients with more work (not to mention more from your existing clients)?

OK, here's the big misnomer. "I don't want business leads from the internet. They are not going to pay our fees." While it may be true that some legal verticals are better for lead generation online than others, you may be looking at websites with the wrong mindset. Getting to the top of Google is only one element to driving new business.

The better way to think about it is to consider your past and existing clients as well as past and existing prospective clients. A good website, blog, newsletter and tasteful advertising can go a long way to driving business back to you again and again.

Having an interactive website and marketing program will target the clients that you want, more so than the small deals that may not be worth your time.

The reality is that most law firms have outdated and ineffective websites that really get nothing accomplished for you and your firm.

It's no surprise that you may find little value in this type of investment. Look, you don't have salespeople out there for you, so maybe having a classy and effective 24/7 sales tool might be a good idea.

I hope this was helpful and that you now understand that this is not an expense, but rather a valuable investment for the future of your firm.

CHAPTER 20

SPECIALIZATION: THE GOOD, BAD AND VERY GOOD

As you know, the Chicago area marketplace is swarming with attorneys looking for their next new client. Will it go to you or to someone who is well-recognized in the legal community as a specialist?

Becoming a "specialist" can be a scary proposition as your messaging and marketing efforts change to accommodate this new direction. The obvious fear is giving up some potential business by speaking and marketing openly about only your new focus.

While most of these fears are not grounded in reality, most generalists are worried about the possible loss that may occur when making the transition.

In working with hundreds of attorneys, we regularly discuss the ups and downs to becoming a specialist. If the timing is right and you are well-prepared, it might be the best way for you to stay relevant, while also growing your practice and obtaining additional financial security.

That being said, it's one thing to be "known" as a

specialist versus "identifying oneself" as a specialist. It's always better to be considered an industry specialist and leader rather than having to advertise that information. In some states, calling yourself a "specialist" is not allowed. Be sure to stay in compliance within your state's or states' guidelines.

Take a moment and think about two of the most successful attorneys you know. Really, close your eyes for five seconds and get their names in your head. I would bet dollars to doughnuts that at least one of the names you thought of was someone who is a specialist. It should come as no surprise that an attorney who builds a reputation around being great at one thing is memorable to you.

The reality is that when you build a reputation in one industry, market or vertical, your practice can grow more quickly than you ever thought possible. Of course, a number of elements need to be in place before taking this leap. Here are a few things to think about before making the switch to becoming a specialist:

1. You need to be the best at what you do.
Whether you are a litigator or a labor and employment attorney, nothing is more important than being skilled at your craft. When thinking about specializing, be sure you have the baseline skills and experience to succeed in one particular area of the law.

It might make sense to get at least two to three clients under your belt in a particular area to test it out and see if specializing in one area makes sense for you.

Achieving notoriety as a specialist may take months or many years to achieve. The important thing is that you eat, sleep and breathe within the space that you've chosen.

A good example of this occurred when I was badly injured in a plane crash back in 1996. That's right, I survived a plane crash. During my recovery from looking like a human pretzel, my father, a now retired attorney, put me on the phone with Bob Clifford of Clifford Law Offices. He chose Bob Clifford because he is well-branded as the leader in aviation and personal-injury litigation. We didn't speak to any other law firms because who could possibly be better?

Being the best at what you do and building a strong reputation around that specialty can make obtaining new clients very easy. However, as you probably know, it takes real effort and conviction to build a specialized practice.

2. Choose the right industry or vertical that's a fit for you.

The easiest and most time effective way to develop a niche is to leverage the work you've already done in one particular area. It may make sense to target specific people, companies or issues that will allow you to draw out more work.

For example, if you've worked with textile manufacturers and enjoy the work, be sure to target other textile companies in your area. You can do a search on Google or LinkedIn to identify the people and companies to call on. Try to leverage your existing clients and strategic relationships to obtain introductions to these business owners if possible.

As an example, you could call up your client in the industry and say, "I know you've been happy with the work I've done for you over the past few years. I am looking to help others in the same area. Who are you friendly with in the textile industry that I should be speaking with as well?"

The key here is to develop a great relationship with your client to ensure that he/she is open to making these types of strategic introductions. Think about it this way. If you had the best dermatologist and someone had a nasty rash, wouldn't you feel great making the introduction?

Another easy way to find the right specialty for you is by asking yourself, "What am I truly passionate about?" If you care about something, it drives you to become more involved.

For example, one of my clients is passionate about animals and is now focusing on working with dog shelters and veterinarians. She joined the shelter's board and is routinely interacting with prospective clients for her practice. She is wowing them with her ability to solve problems and is routinely asked legal questions from the board members.

These inquiries turn into business meetings and eventually new business. She's doing all of this without working harder than before as the new originations roll in.

Finding a niche that you are passionate about can make your legal career much more meaningful and enjoyable. You will also have a greater chance of meeting prospective clients as you will be interacting with them on a more regular basis.

3. Find a space, where there is space.

Be aware of your market and niche and who else may already be there before committing to a specific specialty. While you may have vast experience in commercial real estate for example, there may already be too many lawyers in that area to easily separate yourself from the pack.

Do your research and try to find a segment of real estate that isn't as fully saturated. It might also make sense to branch off into other areas of law to ensure you have your eggs in a few different baskets.

When the recession hit in 2008, many real estate lawyers were hit pretty hard. One of my clients saw this as an opportunity to study estate planning as a backup plan to real estate law. This ended up being a great fit as he was able to leverage his real estate clients and personal contacts to help set up estate plans for everyone he could. Now that real estate is back, he has doubled his book by focusing on both specialties.

By studying the competition, understanding the marketplace and the amount of business generated in a particular area or niche, you can better hedge your bets when selecting a specialty.

4. Look to the future.

A few years ago, I had the great pleasure of interviewing Jerry Maatman of Seyfarth Shaw LLP to learn a little more about his successful practice. One of the key elements to his amazing achievements as an attorney came from his thirst for knowledge within his area of labor and employment. He voraciously read everything he could to better understand what was coming down the pipe to see how he could leverage it to build his practice.

He described in his interview the 1992 legislation for the Americans with Disabilities Act and how he got ahead of the law to be seen as the premier expert on the subject. He effectively packaged a "survival guide" for companies to better deal with the changing laws and regularly spoke on the subject before anyone else.

By being a forward thinker, he locked in his success and was repeatedly hired as the expert on ADA law by some of the largest companies in the country.

Developing a specialization or niche can be a game changer for you as a practicing attorney. For those who are worried about missing other business opportunities because of specializing, who's to say you can't take on new business in other areas?

However, by focusing your outbound marketing on one thing, you'll have the opportunity to build your brand name much more quickly than staying a generalist.

If you do your research, pile up several strong clients and speak with "intent" about your area of focus, only good things will happen for you.

CHAPTER 21

BUILDING BRAND EQUITY REQUIRES THOUGHT AND SIMPLE, BUT IMPORTANT, STEPS

One of the areas attorneys struggle with is building their personal brand equity in the marketplace.

I define personal brand equity, or PBE, as "the value premium that an attorney generates from their perception in the marketplace."

The question you may need to ask yourself is, "What is the current perception of me or my practice in the legal marketplace?" Is it positive, negative or nonexistent? Whatever the case, here are five solid ways that will help you build, repair or grow your current brand in whatever marketplace or practice area you're in.

PBE No. 1 — Google yourself and take action now!

If you're like me, you've Googled yourself at some point. Today, it's more important than ever to do this as potential buyers and referral sources are using Google as a direct resource of information to learn about you.

There may be negative comments or ratings that you're unaware of. In addition, you may find that there's nothing about you, which means you don't exist (to buyers of legal services). On the other hand, type in the name of an attorney whose name you hear regularly. There may be five to 10 pages of search results that clearly demonstrate how this attorney has built his or her PBE.

It has never been more important to make sure your blog post, court wins, published articles and events are all available for the world to see. Failure to load these branding moments into your website or blog are missed opportunities you can't easily get back.

PBE No. 2— Go grassroots: It's time to network.

While it's of critical importance to build your online presence, don't forget to shake hands and kiss some babies along the way. I can't think of too many highly branded rainmaker attorneys that have skipped this step.

Take an hour and research events, conferences and groups that will allow you to meet prospective clients and high-level referral sources. But that's not all! Once you've met them, you need to grab a coffee or lunch, too, on a one-on-one level. Building rapport and finding synergies to refer and work together is a major component of successful brand building.

Try to set a goal for yourself to meet a few solid players each month that will enjoy spreading your name around and talking you up. Think about your favorite restaurant, store or medical practitioner; you probably go out of your way to tell people about how happy you are with them. It's even possible no one has asked you! Just remember, no one wins the race by sitting at a desk.

PBE No. 3 — Seriously, that's your website!

Why do you dress up for work each day? Why not just show up in flip-flops and a tank top? That's exactly what people think about you when they see your terribly outdated and poorly constructed website. Maybe it used to be an afterthought, but today it's critical to how you're viewed in the marketplace. Don't think for a minute that buyers of legal services aren't reviewing your website or bio before calling — or maybe not calling.

It doesn't have to cost a fortune to redo or update your current platform. Holding off on this one investment may be costing you money as potential clients exit the site to move on to other possible options.

The three main reasons people leave your website are website speed, lack of quality information and poor "calls to action." It's important to recognize that it's not about how you use a website, rather it's how your prospective clients, existing clients and potential laterals do.

PBE No. 4 — Get connected, stay connected and add value whenever possible.

You might agree that competition and price pressures in the legal space have never been more severe. My father practiced in the 1980s and 1990s and never had to worry about these things, whereas you should be losing a little sleep over it. That being said, there are so many ways to connect and add value for people in your network, you just have to pay attention and take action.

Three things to focus on are your blog, creating social media posts and maintaining a strong newsletter. These "touch points" can be critical to maintaining your existing base of contacts, clients and potential clients well into the future.

For example, a well-executed post on LinkedIn or Facebook can trigger likes, shares and positive comment that elevate your PBE. The key is to stay top of mind with your network and within the marketplace as a whole. Being visible and providing quality content will prove to be worth its weight in gold as the referrals and repeat business continue to stream in.

PBE No. 5 — The wild card is ... niche!

While this is a subject I've written on before (see the previous chapter), it needs to be summarized here. When the market thinks about the best criminal attorney, aviation attorney or Securities and Exchange Commission attorney, who comes to mind? I'm sure you can name at least one in each area. The reason is because they've won more cases, written more about their area or spoken on their subject more than anyone else.

While the time might not be right for you to have such a definitive focus, it's something worth working toward. It may be hard to believe, but it took me about five years working with attorneys to decide to specialize in the legal profession.

Before that, I had experience working in more than 40 different industries. The key for me was identifying needs in a marketplace that weren't being fulfilled properly. The key before taking the plunge was to gain knowledge and experience while also identifying the opportunity for growth. Once lawyers and law firms became more than 50 percent of my business, it became very clear to me that specialization made sense.

Take the time to review your client base, industries and professions served and what the trends are to determine if it's time to really focus on one thing. Once you've decided your niche, review points one to four above and take aggressive action to build your PBE.

As you continue your journey as an attorney, remember that you don't have to do this alone. There are resources for everything today from software to administrative help to marketing experts (like me!) that can take the nonlegal work off your hands. It may be the best investment you can make in your future as things continue to become more challenging.

CHAPTER 22

HOW TO DRAW MEDIA ATTENTION TO YOUR STORY TIME AND AGAIN

While effective business development is a surefire way to increase your book from year to year, it's important to remember that marketing and public relations can dramatically accelerate your business development efforts.

If you think about a skyscraper rising up to the sky, you must also look down to the base that holds up the behemoth. Taking 15 to 30 minutes a week to focus on growing your brand in the marketplace through positive PR could be an incredibly rewarding endeavor.

"But how do I do that?" you may ask. Well, continue reading Fretzin's five ways to get noticed by the media and you'll find out. Here we go!

Step 1: Control your own story.
You either own your own website, your own LinkedIn profile or your own blog. One way or another you have the ability to write unique and forward-thinking articles to demonstrate your expertise.

While this does take time, you may be practicing for 40-plus years and you will need contact for all those years. The earlier you begin to write or speak, the easier it will be to approach the media or, even better, get singled out and called by them.

Be sure to have a professional-looking presence on anything you do on the web. This will be the first thing any journalist will see before reaching out to you. If you think your website or social media pages look unprofessional or out-of-date, they will think so, too.

One way to find out how you come across is to simply search for yourself online. If things look incomplete, unprofessional and you only have a few search results under your name, you may have some work to do before following the next four steps.

Step 2: Write content that is relevant for today and into the future.

The idea here is to be a "mover and shaker" in your practice area or industry to ensure you get noticed. Be the first one with the story or exclusive to be relevant to the journalist's audience. They want it first, fast and exclusive.

Do your research before writing or speaking to demonstrate that you are a thought leader in your space.

For example, if you're in the estate planning and tax space, you need to study the news and get ongoing feedback regarding the impact of any new tax laws on various business entities or the economy.

Maybe you have a specific twist for small business owners and you can drive that angle to a particular media outlet like Entrepreneur, Inc. magazine or the entrepreneurs' section of The New York Times.

If your story has interesting data points or you see a trend, it could be gold to the journalists you're targeting. Which takes us to our next step.

Step 3: Target your best media contacts.
Journalists today are looking for content — always! There may be a serious win-win outcome when you take the time to introduce yourself and share a new story. Here are a few ways to accomplish this simple task:

• Research on Google or LinkedIn the journalists who have written articles in your city, practice area or industry. It never hurts to follow them on social media and like or comment on their blog posts and articles. Flattery, done with sincerity, doesn't hurt.

• Send an e-mail to introduce yourself. Be sure to provide a link to your website or LinkedIn page and let them know you like their writing. Try referencing a specific article that he or she wrote that hit home for you.

• Provide your best story on a cutting-edge or relevant topic and let the writer know there's more where that came from.

• Be sure to provide your contact information and thank them in advance for their time.

• If you don't hear back, reach out one to two more times with new and interesting stories to see if he or she might bite on something over time.

Step 4: Write news releases to get noticed.
Another way to get found and raise your identity in

the marketplace is to begin writing news releases around new laws, trends or legal battles won. This is rarely done by solos and small firm attorneys but needs to be explored in order to rise to the top. Today there are news release websites that will, for a reasonable investment, blast your story out to hundreds of media outlets.

Step 5: Don't lose touch or your momentum.

Once you've been discovered by a journalist, the most important next step is to simply have one! Go ahead and connect with your new friend on social media so he or she can stay up to speed on you and your posts. Also, be sure to provide exclusives to your journalist so she feels a sense of partnership.

This will help when it's time to reciprocate on a new article and he or she needs a few quotes.

It might even make sense to create a list of journalists and work to communicate on a monthly or quarterly basis. Staying top of mind is half the battle with journalists these days.

I know this may sound a bit daunting, which is why you need to be organized. What can you delegate to your staff and what can only be done by you? Conducting research and executing a written piece or a speaking engagement can be demanding on your time. Focus on topics that will get you noticed and that the media will find interesting to ensure your time is well spent.

PART 3:

Networking

CHAPTER 23

LAW STUDENTS, NETWORKING IS NOW VITAL

Recently, I had the great pleasure of speaking at a Chicago Bar Association event for young attorneys on the topic of networking.

After about 20 minutes, I observed how ravenously everyone was taking notes and the deep level of attentiveness that I was receiving from the participants. While this is not unique to me as a speaker in the legal space, there was something different in the eyes of audience. Fear.

Once the program concluded, I stuck around to chat with the attendees to better understand their mindset. A few of the comments were, "I have no idea how to network and am just trying to put myself out there."

And, "They never taught me any of this in law school." One first-year lawyer even remembered an adjunct professor saying, "If you're not networking, you're not working." The same lawyer then thanked me for my presentation where I explained and demonstrated different ways to actually do it.

Over the past 10 years, I have spoken at a number

of young attorney events, but the fear and confusion on this day was palpable. For more than 200 years, law schools have focused on teaching the law to produce scholarly advocates to protect the rights of his or her clients.

There was never a need to teach networking or how to run a solo practice because lawyers were employed at firms where the primary focus was gaining experience as a lawyer. There was also an abundance of opportunities to get a job.

In economics, we all learned about supply and demand. In the case of the legal space today, the supply of lawyers is overtaking the demand. Especially in the case of the new grads and younger lawyers. With the legal landscape changing, it would only make sense that the law schools must change as well.

One attorney I interviewed was even involved in a 2014 report by the Illinois State Bar Association that revealed that law schools really aren't preparing their students for the challenging legal marketplace that currently exists.

Fortunately, I did uncover that there are some adjunct professors and career services professionals that discuss networking with their students, but it's just not enough. Networking is a learned skill that involves planning and processes to gain traction and ensure positive results.

These skills can be used for the job search, deciding to go solo or as an ongoing activity to grow a book of business. Even the simple skill of asking questions and listening to someone's answers will be critical to a lawyer's ongoing success and sustainability.

Over the past few months, I have been speaking with law schools to discuss this curriculum and its importance to the future of the legal profession. As I continue to develop content and drive these programs forward, here are three core elements that will be included:

Learning how to write a plan

All law school students need to learn how to develop a written plan for finding a job or going out on their own. They say, "Failing to plan is a plan to fail." It is imperative that students learn how to develop and write a plan to better prepare for any eventuality. If the job market were tight, it would be helpful to have developed inside connections to find a good firm or company to work for.

If there were struggles to find the right job, then developing a plan to partner with other solos to develop some business would be valuable.

Whatever the situation, one's ability to develop a plan will be the breakthrough moment for someone wanting a career in the legal space.

Learning how to really use social media

In the age of anytime information and promotion, anyone can use social media to improve their ability to find a job or increase exposure in the marketplace. LinkedIn, for example, allows its users to connect on the site and find inside connections that normally would be hidden.

For example, if we were friends and connected on LinkedIn, you could search through my connections to see the wide variety of general counsels and hiring lawyers that I know.

Asking me for an inside channel into these contacts is infinitely more effective than sending out cold resumes to job postings or firms you are interested in.

Learning the basics of communication, networking

As someone who has killed hundreds of hours by networking inefficiently, I can attest to the importance of structure and processes to follow when networking. These methodologies can be found through books, firm mentors or teachers like myself. For many attorneys, back in school this would be important, because it's not about whom you know anymore but rather how you leverage the relationships with those you know.

Failure to properly give and receive value in a structured way within your network can lead to countless unproductive hours at events and coffee meetings. While it's true that relationships take time, how much time and with whom you invest is in question.

Whether you are currently enrolled in law school, a recent grad or someone who is billing 2,000 hours a year for someone else's clients at your firm, learning to plan and execute on your networking has never been more important.

I know that the law schools today are aware of the need for networking classes, but they just haven't fully committed to the idea. My hope is that with further awareness and forward-thinking deans, graduates will be better equipped to acquire the jobs they are looking for.

CHAPTER 24

GET THE MOST OUT OF YOUR NETWORKING; TAKE THIS TEST AND GRADE YOURSELF

If you've read my book "The Attorney's Networking Handbook," you probably know that I am a big fan of effective networking. I use the word "effective" because networking done improperly is just a huge waste of time.

There are so many elements to networking that we can't possibly cover them in one column, so I thought it would make sense to have you take my survey to better identify where your strengths and weaknesses are, so that you can work to improve upon them.

Take 60 seconds to rate yourself on a scale of 1 to 5 (5 is always) and then we will review ways to improve each focus area. Enjoy!

Question No. 1: When at a networking event, do you focus 100 percent on the person who is speaking with you?

Question No. 2: When at a networking event, do you ask questions to identify how you can help someone else?

Question No. 3: When at a coffee meeting, do you

identify one or two ways you can help or add value for the other person?

Question No. 4: During a one- on-one coffee meeting, do you help the other person identify contacts that would be beneficial to you, versus shying away from this task?

Question No. 5: After your first successful meeting, do you regularly follow up with your best contacts to keep the momentum going?

OK, now rate yourself and total up your score.

If your total was 5 to 10, you have a lot of work ahead to improve your effectiveness.

If your total was 11 to 17, you have minor adjustments to make.

If your total was 18 to 25, you are doing terrific, but there are always new things to learn, so don't get overconfident.

To get you started on the right path, here is one solution to each issue:

Suggestion No. 1: When at a networking event, focus 100 percent on the person who is speaking with you.
Don't push your card at them and stop worrying about impressing people with your canned fancy infomercial.

Instead, ask a few relationship-building business questions to get your new friend talking. For example, if she's an accountant, how about asking, "What do you enjoy about accounting?" or, "How did you get into that line of work?" I'm sure there a story behind their career and discussing it is a great way to build rapport.

Suggestion No. 2: When at a networking event, ask questions to identify how you can help someone else.

Once you've built the rapport as suggested above, ask, "What should I be listening for in a good referral for you?" There are two amazing elements to this question. First, you are being thoughtful to them and possibly helping them in their business development efforts.

Second, you are not committing to providing referrals to this person — yet. Asking isn't offering, which is important because you've only just met this person and shouldn't be providing referrals yet anyway. It may be too soon.

Suggestion No. 3: When at a coffee meeting, you identify one or two ways you can help or add value for the other person.

Now that you know this person better, you want to demonstrate that you have something to offer. If you're listening intently to your new friend, she should be cluing you in on whom she is looking to meet. Take some notes and identify someone worthwhile for her.

Suggestion No. 4: You help the other person identify people that would be beneficial to you,

versus shying away from this task.
This is the one step that good networkers forget. They make referrals, which is terrific, but forget that people need to be led or coached to help you. Take the lead and help her to help you.

Work cooperatively to identify one or two good referrals that would work for you. In addition to walking away from the meeting with some traction, you are also able to test out your new friend to see if her follow-up skills are up to snuff. A win-win!

Suggestion No. 5: You regularly follow up with your best contacts to keep the momentum going after the first meeting was successful.
Another major mistake good networkers make is not staying tightly aligned with the referral partners who you've had success with in the past. It's either a hit-and-run, where you've gotten something and moved on, or you're just busy and forgot that this person has value to you and your business building efforts.

Make a list of your best strategic partners and follow up with them monthly to ensure they stay with you long-term.

The reality is that without some process, thought and methodology behind networking, it can be an unbillable nightmare for any attorney.

The next time you're out networking, try to follow a few of my guidelines and you'll see the improvements in your skills.

CHAPTER 25

NETWORKING TIPS TO BOOST ORIGINATIONS

As you're building or rewriting your business development plan for a new year, it might make sense to look at where improvements and efficiencies can be made. One critical area that's typically overlooked is networking. Any networking event you attend or coffee meeting you conduct can sap away your time at lightning speed. Here are my top five tips for any attorney looking to hit the mark in a new year on the networking front. Enjoy!

Tip 1: Go where the action is. While there are literally hundreds of events you can attend each month, it's of critical importance to focus on going where your best connections will be. Think about the people who need your services and where they might be. Then think about the people who also provide services to those end users and where they might be. That's the place to go.

For example, if you are a commercial litigator, your end clients might be general counsels or CEOs. Where are they when out of the office? Also, what other

Weaver

service providers sell to those general counsels and CEOs? How about middle market CPAs or e-Discovery consultants?

If you keep the end in mind when deciding what events to attend, you may improve your results.

Tip 2: Try talking less, asking more. While it is important to have an infomercial or elevator pitch ready to go, it's even more important to prepare yourself with questions for the people you meet at these events.

The goal is always to get someone else engaged in a conversation where you can learn about her, what she does for a living and find common ground.

I would recommend starting with the easy questions and drive to the more involved. Here are a few questions to choose from:

- "Is this your first time to this event?"
- "This is my first time here, what do you like about this group (or event)?"
- "What type of business are you in?"
- "Do you live in the city or the burbs?"
- "When you're not busy working, what do you do for fun?"
- "What do you enjoy most about your business (career)?"
- "What types of challenges are you seeing in your industry?"
- "What types of people are you most interested in meeting?"
- "What should I be listening for in a good referral

for you?"

Tip 3: Three words: qualify, qualify, qualify. One of the biggest mistakes networkers make is not adequately qualifying the people they meet as it relates to next steps. As an attorney, your time is literally money; so don't agree to meet with everyone you meet.

If someone is a potential client for you, a potential referral partner for you or someone very well connected, there is a direct reason to meet. All other meetings should be taken with great skepticism.

Of course there are exceptions, but choose wisely. This may include "paying it forward" with younger people who you can help with finding a job or launching a new business. Otherwise, you will find that you have just wasted an hour or two with a "nice person" or an annoying salesman who will steal time right away from you.

Tip 4: When you do meet people for coffee, it's best to be prepared. LinkedIn, Facebook and Google are all available at your fingertips; you must use these tools to get prepared to meet someone new. It is simply unacceptable these days to merely show up and say, "So, tell me what do you do?"

Have your talking points and questions ready to go in order to make a good impression. This will ensure that you take the meeting in a positive direction from the get-go.

Tip 5: Always have next steps when it makes sense. Far too often meetings end with the usual, "Great meeting with you. Let's keep our eyes open for one another moving forward." It might be a love fest, but it's not good business acumen for growing originations.

Think about it this way. You meet with a doctor and see that he can make you feel better. Would you leave the next step open or flexible? Of course not! You'd get an appointment to visit again to cure the ailment.

When finishing up a networking meeting when energy is being generated, do your best to set up next steps with your new friend. This could be another meeting, inviting her to a networking group where you belong or inviting her to sit on a panel that you're organizing.

Whatever the case, don't leave a positive meeting without a specific next step forward. Just this one point will dramatically improve your chances of success when networking.

One of my favorite mantras is "There is no failure, only learning." This is so true in networking to ensure you aren't making the same mistakes year after year.

Try to implement at least one of these tips in the new year and you'll see the benefits materialize right before your eyes.

CHAPTER 26

HOW TO PICK UP SOME ACTUAL WORK FROM WORKING A CONFERENCE

When conference season is upon you, it's time to take stock of how you've benefited from these engagements.

As you may already know, these events can be time-consuming and expensive, netting little to no actual new business. Considering all those factors, it seems to defy logic that anyone still goes other than to obtain Continuing Legal Education credit.

Albert Einstein is well known for his definition of insanity, "Doing the same thing over and over and expecting a different result." Is that true for you as it relates to the way you work or don't work a conference?

The real value in attending conferences occurs when its participant is well prepared. Devising a plan that includes being added to the agenda as a presenter, obtaining an attendee list in advance and making a point of scheduling coffee meetings with prospective decision-makers prior to the conference's start are a few of the insider tips you must focus on.

With a well-thought-out plan, proper execution

and prompt follow through, you can change the lackluster conference experiences in your past into results-oriented time where you actually generate new business.

To make my point crystal clear, think about it this way: Would you willingly head into a courtroom for trial without preparing first? Of course not. Just as there are tried-and-true trial preparation tactics you learned in school and on the job, there are some key "success elements" to obtaining new business from attending professional conferences. Here are three "no-brainer" tips to get the most value from any and all conferences.

Tip No. 1: Develop a strong preconference plan or strategy.

• Do background research on past conferences to determine which sessions and receptions might include the best prospects for new clients or strategic partners you would like to meet.

• Have a thorough review of the guest list, if you can obtain it in advance, to understand the background of the attendees. Review the list and place a check next to the people you most want to meet.

• Arrange pre-event meetings (breakfast, lunch or drinks) with some of the prospective attendees. Reach out by telephone or e-mail to schedule these meetings so you'll have a context in place before the event.

• Have discussions with peers, colleagues and friends who've attended the same (or a similar) conference in the past to get the inside scoop on the opportunities available.

• Organize a conversation with the event organizer to get more information about the meeting and to arrange introductions when attending. This can pay big dividends if that person is open to helping you connect at the conference.

• Set goals for the number of contacts you plan to meet each day. Be aggressive with your numbers to ensure you'll meet enough people with whom you'll actually want to follow up after the event.

• Have a completed and well-studied infomercial or elevator pitch to ensure you're seen as focused and polished.

• Use a list of relationship-building and business-focused questions to ask those you meet.

• Practice role-playing to ensure you're ready to ask effective questions that can lead to the development of strong relationships.

Tip No. 2: Be sure to execute your plan at the event.

Thorough planning before the conference matters, but just as important is the next element — execution. When conference day arrives, you'll want to avoid becoming a wallflower or shrinking violet. No matter how introverted you might be, it's critical that you show up and perform with energy.

Advance preparation makes this level of interaction more comfortable and natural. Luckily, there are several tips you can implement to increase your "performance" at any conference.

When meeting someone new, try to be the first to ask questions. In the beginning, you should focus on listening to your contact and learning more about this individual. The more quickly you take in meaningful data, the more quickly you can determine whether this person is someone you want to invest more time with or if you would be better served by moving on and meeting others.

At some point during your conversation it might be appropriate to ask your new contact if any of his or her colleagues at the conference might benefit from meeting you.

Sometimes the person you're talking to may be better suited to connect you to a prospect than to become an actual prospect. Try to understand your contact's business role, position level and circle of influence. These factors can prompt the contact to effectively introduce you to his or her contacts.

In addition, your contact may know about a cocktail reception or other similar event that could put you in a room of possible prospects that you never would have met otherwise. Be open to connections this contact can facilitate.

Don't let a good contact slip away. If you meet someone who strikes you as interesting, well connected or a prospective client, be sure to get his or her card.

Try to make arrangements with this person later. You could do so by saying, "It was really nice meeting you and hearing about all that you do. If you're open to it, I'd really like to meet again and discuss ways we might be able to help one another. How about breakfast tomorrow?"

If the individual isn't available, make sure you collect all of the person's contact information so you can follow up accordingly.

Schedule as many quality meetings with other attendees as possible. You're not building your book of business when you're in your hotel room watching bad movies. Review the one to three days that you're there and commit any free time to holding more one-on-one meetings.

Just as when attending any networking event, label your collected business cards with A, B or C to ensure that you remember whom you met that you thought might be most valuable to your network. This also will help ensure follow-up with the A's and B's directly after the conference.

Connect with your new friends on LinkedIn. This will help you better understand each new contact's background and who else they know. This little step can make your follow-up meetings even more interesting.

Schedule follow-up calls with attendees before you leave the conference. If you're speaking with someone and it makes sense to speak again, pull out your calendar and schedule the time while that contact is right in front of you. This is better than getting back to them when they might be too busy to take your call.

Speak to the people sitting next to you at each meal and workshop. Sometimes the best opportunities happen when you least expect it. You can easily double or triple your chances of meeting a valuable connection just by doing this one thing.

Tip No. 3: Seize your window of opportunity after the conference.
The third element of being successful at a conference happens after you leave. Remember that, when developing new business, you typically have a short, 48-hour window to follow up to get the best possible results. You'll need to start moving when you return to the office.

Some of my attorney clients will wait weeks before making follow-up phone calls. Don't leave to chance that your new contact has a good memory; you can lose the chance to make a connection with even those who do once they get back to their daily grind.

Additionally, communicating early is important because the conference's energy is still fresh for your prospects. If you're looking for one way to help make a follow-up call or e-mail stick, say the following to a valuable connection before leaving the conference, "I'd really like to follow up with you to continue this conversation. Is it best to reach you through e-mail or just to call?" This way you also ensure you'll be touching base using the contact's preferred manner of communication.

Success tactics for following up with potential strategic partners
• Review the person's LinkedIn profile to see your

second-degree and his or her first-degree connections. This will help you better qualify possible introductions you might ask your new contact to make.

• Develop questions to better understand the individual's business, including your contact's target market. Try to think of connections you could foster for this new acquaintance. Always remember that networking is a two-way street.

• Ask questions to understand whether meeting face-to-face or by telephone to follow up makes more sense. Disqualifying potential contacts is just as important as qualifying them and doing so can conserve your valuable time.

• Set a "loose" agenda for your next meeting to ensure both parties will get value and walk away with concrete plans to help one another.

Success tactics for following up with prospective clients

• LinkedIn is an excellent tool for following up with new contacts. Look for common first-degree connections to determine connections you have in common. This helps with relationship building and finding natural affinities. Then you can reach out to your new friend with a personal message and invite him or her to a lunch, drinks or a follow-up call.

• Take a few minutes to develop rapport. It's fine to talk about the conference or acquaintances you may have in common with this person.

Hopefully, you jotted some quick notes about your new connections while still at the conference so that you have topics to chat about afterward that you can tie back to your initial conversation.

For example, compare notes with your contact about who you thought was the best conference speaker or which was the best reception you attended.

• When you get to the phone call, be alert for, and even gently probe for, any legal issues or problems with existing vendors your prospect might be having. Anytime someone shares this type of information with you, this is an opening for you to move forward and help the person improve the situation.

If you do identify problems you could ask what issues in particular are causing the contact and his or her company the most frustration. Make sure you know he or she is interested in discussing this with you before asking this question.

• Schedule a full meeting during this follow-up call. The goal isn't to close a sale, but rather to gain commitment to the next step: a full meeting.

• Try to understand whether your contact is a decision-maker for the company or newer counsel. If not the main decision-maker, ask subtle questions about the contact's business to find out who the decision-makers are.

• Set an agenda for your meeting. This will set up the meeting to accomplish both your goals and those of your contact.

Keep in mind that relationship building takes time. Unless your new contact has needs for your services, it might be months or years before the business comes your way. The good news is that with strong relationship building skills, questioning skills and follow-up, you have a much better chance of landing the business than if you did none of the above.

Like with any good story, there's a beginning, middle and end. Think of each conference the same way. There's planning, execution and follow-through needed to have a happy ending with your conferences.

I'm sure if you think back to the last conference you attended, you'll see a number of my suggestions would ultimately have filled the gaps that existed without any processes being utilized. Use these methodologies, and you'll experience a dramatic shift in your results, which is the name of the game.

CHAPTER 27

HOW TO GIVE YOURSELF A GIFT DURING THE HOLIDAYS: WHAT ABOUT A FEW CLIENTS?

When you think about the holidays, what runs through your head? Is it the department store music? Is it the rush to find that once in a lifetime deal? Or is it the end-of-the-year gut check gnawing away at your psyche, questioning whether you've made good use of your time this year in building your law practice?

In speaking and working with hundreds of attorneys, I've heard my share of holiday frustrations around managing one's time. Mostly it's misperceptions about the holidays, which I call the Santa Claus Blues. Even though the holidays may bring cheer to many, it brings nervousness and potential despair to the attorney looking for some year-end business. Some of the things I hear include:

• "Everyone is away on vacation, so no one will meet with me."

• "These holiday parties are all the same- a huge waste of time."

• "I'm too busy (with the shortened month) to develop new business."

While these statements might be true for you in the past, I'd like to offer some suggestions for improving your outlook this holiday season.

Steve's Holiday Tip No. 1: December is the perfect time to schedule meetings.

While many attorneys believe that everyone is away on vacation, the reality is that most are sticking around. American Automobile Association research suggests that only one-third of the U.S. population will travel far from home this holiday season. Most trips will be within 50 miles. This relates directly to my point that there are loads of opportunities to get in front of clients, strategic partners and friends this December to develop new business.

I would suggest making a short list of 10 to 15 people to call to set up a lunch or coffee meeting. Think about your best-connected relationships and write their names down. It will only take a few minutes. Once you have the list completed, open your calendar and schedule an hour this week to make these calls. Do yourself a favor and take 10 minutes to do this directly after reading my article.

In my experience, you will be able to schedule three or four meetings, while also leaving another 10 messages to people who will call you back later today or tomorrow. The goal here is to schedule five to 10 meetings in December that you normally wouldn't be scheduling. When properly executed, these meetings will open doors for upselling, cross-marketing and quality introductions to new clients.

Steve's Holiday Tip No. 2: Effectively work a holiday party.
While it might be fun to attend holiday parties for the food, drink and merriment, you may be missing opportunities to uncover new potential clients. This isn't to say that you need to be a shark circling its prey. Rather, you might think about three things to help make your time more useful during the party.

The first thing I recommend is communicating with the host the specific people you would like to meet while at the party. Simply call the host or person who invited you and ask, "While I'm at your party, who are some good people I should be sure to meet?"

Once she's given you a few names, follow it up with, "That's great. Would you mind walking me over to them during the party to introduce me personally?" Just a few extra steps can make the event more worthwhile.

The second suggestion would be to prepare a few good business questions to ask when meeting new people. This might take away the awkwardness of what you should and shouldn't say or help eliminate a lull in the conversation. As you know, people love talking about themselves. All you're doing is directing the conversation to better understand their business or personal life at a higher level. A few questions that I've used include:
- What type of business are you in?
- How did you get into it?
- What does the future hold for your industry?

• What are some of the challenges that you face on a day-to-day basis (my personal favorite)?

It's also a good idea to ask one of these questions, listen and then ask a deeper follow-up question. The point here is that by focusing on the other person first, you not only understand if he or she might be a good prospective client or strategic partner, but you might disqualify the person as someone you should move away from quickly. Moving someone into the "no" column can be just as valuable for your time as moving someone forward to a "yes."

My last suggestion is to follow up quickly with the people you've met. Again, we might be inclined to wait because of the holidays. However, there's nothing wrong with following up the next day and trying to schedule a meeting in December or early next year. By following up right away you show interest and good communication skills, and it's more likely that people will remember you.

In some cases, I've built rapport to the point where we scheduled an appointment on the spot for the following week. Both parties were open to taking out our phones and getting the meeting on the books. Sometimes you just need to make the suggestion.

Steve's Holiday Tip No. 3: A failure to plan is a plan to fail.

One of the best ways to utilize any downtime during the holiday season is to take stock of what happened this past year. Really look at your activities and the corresponding results. Then ask yourself the following questions:

• How many clients did I meet with this past year? Did I do anything to ensure client satisfaction or loyalty? Was I able to open dialogs with clients relating to upselling, cross-marketing or asking for introductions?

• Who were my best strategic partners and referral sources? What industries are they in? How did I give back to my best referral sources? What did I do to find more strategic partners this year?

• What did I do to obtain new business that worked and what didn't?

• What did I do this year to improve my business development skills?

• Do I have a written plan for next year?

Based on your answers you either have a Cheshire grin on your face, or you're beginning to perspire. If it's the latter, don't fret. It's only December and you can still make plans to improve things for next year.

One important element in planning for next year is developing a solid SWOT analysis. This is an old-school marketing acronym, but it still works well today. SWOT stands for one's internal strengths and weaknesses as well as their external opportunities and threats. We can break this down further by defining them and providing a few examples of each.

Strengths: What are your strengths as a person and as a legal practitioner? You are a socially charged person with a huge network; you have the uncanny ability to read people; you have written 10 articles on one legal subject, and no one knows it better.

Weaknesses: What are your weaknesses as a person or legal practitioner? You are highly introverted and shy; you are new to practicing law and don't have much experience; you are a generalist, and no one really knows what you do.

Opportunities: What opportunities are open to you in the marketplace? You are specializing in a new area of the law, such as medical marijuana; you see an opening in a networking group where you will be the only lawyer included; you have hundreds of clients and haven't tapped into cross-marketing yet.

Threats: What are the threats to you in the marketplace? You are a residential real estate attorney, and closings are all driven by the lowest rate; competition in your area is out of control: There are 100 attorneys for every deal; your firm's name is not well known.

Going through your SWOT analysis and asking yourself the tough questions can be a truly eye-opening experience. By being honest with yourself, you can realize what, why and how to improve yourself and your situation for next year.

Einstein said the definition of insanity is doing the same things over and over again and expecting a different result. Make the important changes and take responsibility for last year's successes and failures.

The key to having a successful year-end is to not sit on your hands and let the time pass. December can be a very productive month if you focus on planning and setting some quality meetings — with quality people.

Part 4:
Practice Management

CHAPTER 28

INVESTING IN BUSINESS DEVELOPMENT — A LAW FIRM'S CONUNDRUM

When it comes to internal attorney growth, many law firms struggle to move the needle and help their senior associates and partners effectively grow their books of business.

Many firms invest millions of dollars a year developing teams of former attorneys and industry experts who truly desire to help their attorneys to get ahead, yet have little results to show from their investment. Why is this?

The easiest way to explain a firm's shortcomings around internal business development growth is to look at what it really takes to become a lawyer in the first place. Let me break it down for you.

As you know, to be a great lawyer you need to work hard as an undergrad and graduate with a solid GPA. Then you must excel in law school for three years, learn the theory of law and pass the bar. If that wasn't enough, it takes years of experience to truly learn the law and how it applies to one or more practice areas. While I'm not an attorney myself, we can all agree that this isn't easy and it doesn't happen without a serious commitment.

Now, what does it take to become an effective business developer? This may be the dirty little secret that law firm leaders do not want to hear. Becoming a rainmaker can take a similar effort and formal education as becoming a successful lawyer.

Really, though, why should it be different? My entire day, every day, is working with attorneys who have no business to speak of and also attorneys who have million-dollar books. What do they have in common? No formal education in business development.

It really isn't fair to assume that business development can be easily learned through trial and error. Imagine not going to law school and walking into a courtroom to try a case. That would be pretty crazy, right?

When time is money, making mistakes in business development can cost more than you would believe. One of my clients invested hundreds of hours a year into business development, never achieving the results that he desired.

He attended all the events and conferences, gave presentations all over the country and made enthusiastic pitches to prospective clients. All that, and the growth still wasn't there. Without a formal education and coaching, it's very difficult to become a great business developer.

Here are three suggestions to help law firms make better decisions on their business development initiatives:

Tip No. 1: Do your research

If you're looking for programming that gets results, ask your peers and search online to find the coaches, trainers and consultants that have gotten real results for their clients. Results will not happen in a one-day retreat or seminar. Real results take time, energy and commitment to succeed.

Tip No. 2: Don't invest in everyone the same way

While you want to be supportive and help everyone, there should be levels established to provide assistance where it's appropriate. Before investing, consider the attorney's seniority, potential, interest and commitment when deciding what program to engage each attorney in.

For example, first-year attorneys need smaller programs that focus on networking and building relationships. More seasoned and coachable attorneys may need training and coaching that may be more intensive, sometimes ranging from six months to a year.

Time management, networking and selling legal services are all processes that can be learned over time. It might make sense to handpick some of your best and brightest and invest in them. They are the firm's future and when done properly, grooming these folks can be a better investment than bringing over a lateral.

Tip No. 3: Program development is critical to success

When searching out a resource for business development or developing a platform internally, the key to success can rest on the program's ability to provide structure for the attorneys selected into the program.

As you know already, winging it is not a process. Attorneys need specific steps to follow and appropriate language to use to obtain real results. There should be materials and a sound curriculum to accompany the coaching and training to running a professional program.

Whether you select an outside resource or build something internally, be sure to use processes that have been proven in the legal space and that are up to date with the current state of the legal marketplace.

The harsh reality is that it's the business of law, which means that business development education is now as fundamentally vital as being a great lawyer.

As you know, you can't practice the law without clients to work with. The good news is that business development training and coaching is becoming more available and relevant than ever before.

If you begin to think about it more as an advanced education or degree that is necessary for success, it may be easier pill to swallow.

CHAPTER 29

GETTING THE RIGHT LATERAL IS NOT EASY; DEVELOP A PLAN AND STICK WITH IT

It's no secret in the legal community that firms are investing huge sums to win over attorneys who own large books of business.

It's been a proven method of growth that corporations do every day to expand and dominate the marketplace. The math is simple. Find a lawyer or group of lawyers with millions in business and acquire the businesses they control.

Unfortunately, there are two substantial missteps that are occurring when choosing to add laterals to the firm's team.

Initially, firms struggle to identify, interview and select the best candidates that would "fit" neatly into the firm. And subsequently, there's no specific process to effectively onboard the laterals to ensure a successful transition.

When added together, many firms are bringing in the wrong people from the get-go or finding the right people but leaving them on their own to figure things out.

Either way, this is a huge investment that isn't paying off properly for the firm or the newly acquired attorney. While the solution can't be expressed fully in my column, I would like to share some thoughts from my 20-plus years in recruiting, business and sales.

Here are two critical tips that I know can change the game for everyone involved:

Create a process for interviewing that is proven.

When taking a case to trial, you probably have steps that you follow which have been proven effective for you in the past. You may have even learned these steps from a mentor or someone who knew the ropes before you did.

Interviewing is the same in many respects. There must be steps that are followed to obtain the greatest result for everyone involved. The firm's future and the attorney being sought after are both at risk here, so try these alternatives:

• Steal ideas and processes from the most successful people you know. This may include former managing partners, human resources directors and even the recruiters you may be using.

• Create a specific series of steps that guides the candidate through the interview process. Start with a resume and online review (LinkedIn, Facebook, etc.) and move things to a phone call. If that goes well, continue the process forward making each step more in-depth as you go.

• Use science to ensure your gut is on the right

track. There are some very sophisticated assessments which will help you better understand the candidate's behaviors, personality, intelligence and social skills. Use these assessments as a way to disqualify attorneys that won't fit the job or culture within your firm.

• Create "telling questions" that are open-ended to get the most from the interview. Have two to three highly successful and experienced attorneys or executives conduct the interviews to get a variety of opinions on the candidate. Running an interview in an unstructured manner will lead to a poor hiring decision every time.

Set up a structured onboarding plan for new laterals.

While many firms think that they have this in place, they don't. I regularly hear stories of the million-dollar lateral that is brought in and then told, "Here's your office and your phone, let us know if you need anything else." What?!

Execution on an effective onboarding plan will make or break the huge investment that the firm has just made. It has multiple steps and layers that help ensure success for the attorney brought into the firm. This might include:

• Assigning one executive committee member to be responsible for the lateral. This person would invest time over the first 90 days introducing the new attorney around and making him comfortable with the team. This also helps get the cross-marketing efforts off the ground.

- Setting up a written plan for the onboarding and training process. Creating a predictable and manageable plan for the attorney makes a world of difference. Most attorneys thrive when structure is provided.

This plan would break down the first week, month and quarter of the attorney's time as it relates to internal and external activities. The worst feeling is when the lateral has been around for 90 days and nothing has been accomplished to integrate him into the firm.

- Most importantly, it is critical to assist the new lateral in bringing over and growing his book of business. If he has sold you on the million-dollar book, that must be realized for this to work for both parties. Be sure to find external or internal training and support to get your new attorney rocking in the right direction. Everyone loses when originations that are expected aren't realized.

If you do that math on just one broken lateral, the numbers can be staggering. This could be the million-dollar book that isn't realized, the recruiter's fees or the unbillable time that was invested and lost forever.

Whatever the case, creating an actual plan and process can save the day — and is the bottom line for firms that think more strategically than in the past.

CHAPTER 30

DARWINISM IN THE MARKETPLACE: WORKER BEES AND DREAMERS

What would Darwin say about an attorney's ability to survive in business today? Which species of lawyer will evolve and which will become extinct?

"Survival of the fittest" is a phrase relating to competition for survival or predominance. Currently, there are three species of attorneys competing for survival in the marketplace.

The first is the worker bee attorney. This class of attorney is a skilled professional who bills a tremendous number of hours and primarily assists the busier attorneys at the firm.

The second type is the rainmaker attorney. This is the big hitter who brings in the whales and drives business into the firm. Without this type of attorney, the mid-market and larger firms wouldn't exist. They are also difficult to replace when exiting the practice of law.

The last type of attorney is what I refer to as the "dreamer." This motivated class of attorney envisions becoming the rainmaker someday, but doesn't typically have the knowledge, skills or discipline to make the conversion.

While the worker bee's future is at risk based on the hours regularly handed off, the dreamer has the opportunity to not only survive but also thrive in growing a successful and prosperous practice. He or she sees the road ahead and understands that building a book of business is mission critical to a sustainable future.

So, who will survive or become extinct in a harsher and overly commoditized industry? The answers to these questions are being answered every day in the news as law firms break apart, merge and new law school graduates struggle to find jobs.

It has never been more obvious that the attorneys without books of business find themselves wondering what the future may hold.

There are a number of approaches that attorneys can use to ensure future security and freedom in their practice. Here are four solid strategies for any attorney aiming to thrive in a competitive marketplace:

Utilize your strongest relationships for introductions.

They say in business, "It's all about who you know." The truth today is a little more specific than that. It's really about "How you leverage the people you know."

Let's take a moment to look at the importance of leveraging existing clients and strategic partners to obtain more business. As I'm sure you recognize, there are no better avenues to drive new business than a referral from a happy client. That being said, many attorneys don't ask for referrals due to the fear of coming across pushy or salesy or desperate.

Mainly, this is what I call "head trash." The reality is that your client is probably happy to refer you, but just hasn't been asked. Most attorneys feel awkward asking for introductions primarily due to a lack of a proper process and appropriate language to get the desired response. While there may be some fear in leveraging these relationships, it is crucial to developing a bigger book of business.

The first step is to clearly identify your best referral sources and simply ask them to lunch, coffee or dinner. Be prepared to discuss ways in which you can add value for them to ensure this is not a one-way street.

A few examples of adding value for a client during this lunch would be to provide her or him with a quality introduction to someone that can add value to his or her business. This could be a potential client, vendor or consultant.

Another way to make it easier is to first help solve a problem that is unrelated to the law. For example, ask questions about her family or other interests she has.

You might find she's looking to remodel her home and needs a good contractor. If you know one, offer the name. Whether the contact is a client or a good strategic partner, invest time with him. In addition to building goodwill, you will have a better opportunity to obtain a referral or uncover an opportunity to cross-market. In times like these, you are always better off utilizing existing relationships to find the most qualified new ones.

Work to become a specialist.
Bar rules state that an attorney cannot call herself a "specialist." But when you are a true specialist, you won't need to label yourself as such. The market around you will handle that directly for you.

With more than 1.3 million attorneys in the United States, competition has never been fiercer. When survival is a factor in the marketplace, nothing compares to being well known and respected in a niche area of law. Take a moment and think about some of the attorneys you refer. In many cases, it's because something came across your desk and you knew the best person to hand it off to.

Many attorneys have shared concerns with me about focusing their practice and the possibility of missing opportunities that don't fall under their realm. The reality is that the short-term gain of staying a generalist will not outweigh the long-term benefit of becoming famous in one specific niche of the law or a specific industry.

There are two easy ways to find a niche that might work for you. First, think about the area of law that you have become really talented in. Second, think about something that you are very passionate about.

For example, a very talented estate planning attorney who also has a passion for charity could become successful working with non-profits. Or a health care attorney who truly cares about the elderly could focus in the eldercare law.

Take some time and research the industries or related niches where you have an interest. Try to better understand how many attorneys have a similar focus in that niche and how crowded the space may be in your particular locale.

Lawyers that are known for particular areas are memorable and become highly referable by their peers. By focusing and eventually leveraging the experience of working in a niche, attorneys can build a little empire by concentrating in one area.

Embrace technology

Take a moment and think about how far technology has taken us in the past 20 years. We have gone from fax machines and corded phones to memory sticks and smart phones in what seems like a blink of an eye. One of the best and most underutilized tools from the past 10 years is LinkedIn. Most attorneys I work with tell me, "I'm on there, but not really using it." While I understand that social media is scary and can be seen as a tremendous waste of time, there are some silver linings within the gray cloudy mass.

The truth is that most social media platforms are not right for most attorneys. However, LinkedIn may be the exception as it is widely known by its successful users as the best networking tool ever created. There are three key elements to being successful in leveraging this technology to your advantage.

First, you must develop a solid profile. People are watching you and you may not even realize it. Having a profile that is incomplete or inaccurate can hurt your image. It's similar to a resume that is riddled with typos. Invest 20 minutes and look at some creative and more elaborate LinkedIn profiles of your peers. Mimic what they are doing and update your profile until you reach 100 percent complete.

Second, develop an appropriate strategy for what you are trying to accomplish. If you aren't looking to meet or talk with anyone, don't set up a profile and stay off the site. If you are looking to get out there and promote your expertise, connect with the people who can help you advance your interests.

If you're like me and want the world to see you, be more open to allowing a variety of new people to connect with you.

That being said, I don't want to connect with total strangers. Unless they write and tell me why connecting would be of value, I will usually not accept their request to connect.

The third and most important element of using LinkedIn is to use it to leverage your best connections to get quality introductions. The greatest benefit of this platform is being able to actually see who your connections know.

For example, let's say I have a client who has become a friend. I can go into her profile and pull up all of her connections. If there is one that seems like the perfect introduction for me, I could simply ask her what she thinks.

Based on her response, I would follow up and ask her to make a call on my behalf to her friend and introduce me. It's just that simple. I have been teaching LinkedIn for years, and it's been a proven winner for new lead generation for attorneys.

Find help

If you were to take a trip through Africa, from the bottom of the continent to the top, would you do that alone? How many people are able to become an expert at playing an instrument without a teacher? Business development is a learned skill.

If you fall into the dreamer category and want to build your book of business today, it should be mission critical that you ask for help. This might be a mentor internal to your firm or an ally in your marketing department.

Another option is to try to find an experienced lawyer outside of your firm who might be willing to invest some time in helping you develop some skills or a specialization.

One obvious choice is to research and select a coach or consultant that can help you directly in growing your book. There are many qualified people that you can hire to assist you. My only word of warning is to thoroughly research and vet the right person for you. Research him or her online and review recommendations on LinkedIn. Speak with his past clients to ensure he is driving results to the clients' book of business.

While there are many ways to improve your law practice during turbulent times, most people are moving along slowly, as if a car crash is holding up traffic. The idea behind Darwinism for the legal business is simple. The fittest will survive and the weakest will die. Try to utilize your relationships, become specialized and get whatever help you might need to ensure success.

ABOUT THE AUTHOR

Steve Fretzin is the President of FRETZIN, Inc., a legal business development and marketing company founded in 2004. He was driven into the legal industry during the recession of 2008 when attorneys began calling him for help. While not an attorney himself, Steve has worked with thousands of attorneys in most practice areas. Steve is 100% committed to his client's success and works diligently each day to ensure they are achieving their goals of financial and personal freedom.

In addition to publishing "Sales-Free Selling" and "The Attorney's Networking Handbook," Steve has been featured in Crain's, The Chicago Tribune, WGN radio, NBC news and is a regular monthly columnist for the Chicago Daily Law Bulletin.

In addition to enjoying free time with his wife Lisa and son Andrew, Steve loves to eat healthy food, travel and play platform tennis. (Look it up on YouTube!) Steve's mantras in life are to control what is controllable and to not be afraid of new experiences.